1000
THINGS
YOU SHOULD KNOW ABOUT

SCIENCE

1000 THINGS YOU SHOULD KNOW ABOUT

SCIENCE

John Farndon

Miles Kelly
PUBLISHING

**This edition first published in 2003 for
Books are Fun**

First published in 2000 by
Miles Kelly Publishing,
Bardfield Centre, Great Bardfield, Essex, CM7 4SL, U.K.
Copyright © Miles Kelly Publishing 2000, 2003

2 4 6 8 10 9 7 5 3 1

Library of Congress Cataloging-in-Publication Data on file
at the Library of Congress

ISBN 1-902947-26-6

Editorial Director: Anne Marshall
Editors: Amanda Learmonth, Jenni Rainford
Assistant: Liberty Newton
Americanization: Cindy Leaney
Written and designed by: John Farndon and Angela Koo

Printed in China

CONTENTS

KEY

 Matter

 Chemicals and materials

 Electricity, magnetism, and radiation

 The frontiers of science

 Technology

Energy, force, and motion

Computers

- **Part of a computer's** memory is microchips built in at the factory and known as ROM, or read-only memory. ROM carries the basic working instructions.

- **RAM** (random-access memory) consists of microchips that receive new data and instructions when needed.

- **Data can also** be stored as magnetic patterns on a removable disk, or on the laser-guided bumps on a CD (compact disk) or DVD (digital versatile disk).

- **At the heart** of every computer is a powerful

◄ *Computers are developing so rapidly that models from the 1990s already look dated.*

microchip called the central processing unit, or CPU.

- **The CPU** works things out, within the guidelines set by the computer's ROM. It carries out programs by sending data to the right place in the RAM.

- **Computers** store information in bits (binary digits), either as 0 or 1.

- **The bits 0 and 1** are equivalent to the OFF and ON of electric current flow. Eight bits make a byte.

- **A kilobyte** is 1,000 bytes; a megabyte (MB) is 1,000,000 bytes; a gigabyte (GB) is 1,000,000,000 bytes; a terabyte (TB) is 1,000,000,000,000 bytes.

- **A CD can hold** about 600 MB of data—about 375,000 pages of ordinary text.

> ★ STAR FACT ★
> The US Library of Congress's 70 million books could be stored in 25 TB of computer capacity.

Turning forces

- **Every force** acts in a straight line. Things move around because of a "turning effect."

- **A turning effect** is a force applied to an object that is fixed or pivots in another place, called the fulcrum.

- **In a door** the fulcrum is the hinge.

- **The size of a turning force** is known as the moment.

▲ *Interlocking gear wheels are used in a huge range of machines, from cars to cameras. The wheels transmit movements and control their speed and size.*

- **The farther from the fulcrum** that a force is applied, the bigger the moment is.

- **A lever** makes it much easier to move a load by making use of the moment (size of turning force).

- **A first-class lever,** such as pliers or scissors, has the fulcrum between the effort and the load; a second-class lever, such as a screwdriver or wheelbarrow, has the load between the effort and the fulcrum; a third-class lever, such as your lower arm or tweezers, has the effort between the load and the fulcrum.

- **Gears are sets of wheels** of different sizes that turn together. They make it easier to cycle uphill, or for a car to accelerate from a standstill, by spreading the effort over a greater distance.

- **The gear ratio** is the number of times that the wheel doing the driving turns the wheel being driven.

- **The larger the gear ratio** the more the turning force is increased, but the slower the driven wheel turns.

Archimedes

- **Archimedes** (c.287–212BC) was a great scientist. He created the sciences of mechanics and hydrostatics.

- **Archimedes** was a Greek who lived in the city of Syracuse, Sicily. His relative, Hieron II, was king of Syracuse.

- **Archimedes' screw** is a simple pump invented by Archimedes. It scoops up water with a spiral device that turns inside a tube. It is still used in the Middle East.

- **To help defend** Syracuse against Roman attackers in 215BC, Archimedes invented many war machines. They included an awesome "claw"—a grappling crane that could lift whole galleys from the water and sink them.

- **Archimedes** was killed by Roman soldiers when collaborators let the Romans into Syracuse in 212BC.

- **Archimedes** analyzed levers mathematically. He showed that the load you can move with a particular effort is in exact proportion to its distance from the fulcrum.

- **Archimedes discovered** that things float because they are thrust upward by the water.

- **Archimedes' principle** shows that the upthrust on a floating object is equal to the weight of the water that the object pushes out of the way.

- **Archimedes** realized he could figure out the density, or specific gravity, of an object by comparing the object's weight to the weight of water it pushes out of a jar when completely submerged.

- **Archimedes** used specific gravity to prove that King Hieron's crown was not made of pure gold.

▶ The story says that Archimedes came up with the idea of measuring specific gravity while in the bath. He was so thrilled that he ran into the streets shouting "Eureka!" (meaning "I've got it").

Magnetism

- **Magnetism** is the invisible force between materials such as iron and nickel. Magnetism attracts or repels.

- **A magnetic field** is the area around a magnet inside which its magnetic force can be detected.

- **An electric current** creates its own magnetic field.

- **A magnet** has two poles: a north pole and a south pole.

- **Like (similar) poles** (e.g. two north poles) repel each other; unlike poles attract each other.

★ **STAR FACT** ★
One of the world's strongest magnets is at the Lawrence Berkeley National Laboratory. Its field is 250,000 times stronger than the Earth's.

- **The Earth** has a magnetic field that is created by electric currents inside its iron core. The magnetic north pole is close to the geographic North Pole.

- **If left to swivel freely**, a magnet will turn so that its north pole points to the Earth's magnetic north pole.

- **The strength of a magnet** is measured in teslas. The Earth's magnetic field is 0.00005 teslas.

- **All magnetic materials** are made up of tiny groups of atoms called domains. Each one is like a mini-magnet with north and south poles. When material is magnetized, millions of domains line up.

◀ The glowing skies above the poles are called auroras. They are created by the way the Earth's magnetic field channels electrically charged particles from the Sun down into the atmosphere.

New materials

- **Synthetic materials** are materials created by humans, such as plastics.

- **Many synthetic materials** are polymers—substances with long chains of organic molecules made up from lots of identical smaller molecules (monomers).

- **Some polymers** are natural, such as the plant fiber, cellulose.

▲ Snowboards are made from composites such as Kevlar, which combine lightness with strength.

> **! NEWS FLASH !**
> New "smart" materials might change their properties in response to conditions.

- **The first synthetic polymer** was Parkesine, invented by Alexander Parkes in 1862. The first successful synthetic polymer was celluloid, invented by John Hyatt in 1869 and soon used for photographic film.

- **Nylon** was the first fully synthetic fiber. It is a polymer created by Wallace Carothers of Du Pont in the 1930s.

- **PVC** is polyvinyl chloride, a synthetic polymer .

- **Composites** are new, strong, light materials created by combining a polymer with another material.

- **Carbon-reinforced plastic** consists of tough carbon fibers set within a polymer.

- **Kevlar** is a composite developed by Du Pont in 1971. It is made from nylon-like fibers set within a polymer.

Salts and soaps

- **Some soaps** are natural; all detergents are synthetic.

- **All soaps and detergents** clean with a "surfactant."

- **Surfactants** are molecules that attach themselves to particles of dirt on dirty surfaces and lift them away.

- **Surfactants** work because one part of them is hydrophilic (attracted to water) and the other is hydrophobic (repelled by water).

- **The hydrophobic tail** of a surfactant digs its way into the dirt; the other tail is drawn into the water.

- **Soaps** increase water's ability to make things wet by reducing the surface tension of the water.

- **Soap** is made from animal fats or vegetable oil combined with chemicals called alkalis, such as sodium or potassium hydroxide.

- **Most soaps** include perfumes, colors, and germicides (germ-killers) as well as a surfactant.

- **The Romans used** soap over 2,000 years ago.

- **Detergents** were invented in 1916 by a German chemist called Fritz Gunther.

▼ Surfactant molecules in soap lift dirt off dirty surfaces.

The hydrophobic tail dips into the dirt

The hydrophilic tail is pulled by the water

Surfactant molecules lift particles of dirt away

Musical sound

◀ In stringed instruments different notes—that is, different frequencies of vibrations—are achieved by varying the length of the strings.

- **Like all sounds,** musical sounds are made by something vibrating. However, the vibrations of music occur at very regular intervals.

- **The pitch** of a musical note depends on the frequency of the vibrations.

- **Sound frequency** is measured in hertz (Hz)—that is, cycles or waves per second.

> **★ STAR FACT ★**
> A song can shatter glass if the pitch of a loud note coincides with the natural frequency of vibration of the glass.

- **Human ears** can hear sounds as low as about 20Hz and up to around 20,000Hz.

- **Middle C** on a piano measures 262Hz. A piano has a frequency range from 27.5 to 4,186Hz.

- **The highest singing voice** can reach the E above a piano top note (4,350Hz); the lowest note is 20.6Hz.

- **A soprano's voice** has a range from 262 to 1,046Hz; an alto from 196 to 698Hz; a tenor from 147 to 466Hz; a baritone from 110 to 392Hz; a bass from 82.4 to 294Hz.

- **Very few sounds** have only one pitch. Most have a fundamental (low) pitch and higher overtones.

- **The science of vibrating strings** was first figured out by Pythagoras 2,500 years ago.

▶ In most brass and woodwind instruments, such as a tuba, different frequencies are achieved by varying the length of the air column inside.

Lasers

- **Laser light** is a bright artificial light. It creates an intense beam that can punch a hole in steel. A laser beam is so straight and narrow that it can hit a mirror on the Moon.

- **The name "laser"** stands for light amplification by stimulated emission of radiation.

- **Laser light** is even brighter for its size than the Sun.

▲ The amazingly tight intense beam of a laser is used in a huge number of devices, from CD players to satellite guidance systems.

- **Laser light** is the only known "coherent" source of light. This means the light waves are not only all the same wavelength (color), but they are also perfectly in step.

- **Inside a laser** is a tube filled with gases, such as helium and neon, or a liquid or solid crystal such as ruby.

- **Lasers work** by bouncing photons (bursts of light) up and down the tube until they are all traveling together.

- **Lasing begins** when a spark excites atoms in the lasing material. The excited atoms emit photons. When the photons hit other atoms, they fire off photons too. Identical photons bounce backward and forward between mirrors at either end of the laser.

- **Gas lasers** such as argon lasers give a lower-powered beam. It is suitable for delicate work such as eye surgery.

- **Chemical lasers** use liquid hydrogen fluoride to make intense beams for weapons.

- **Some lasers** send out a continuous beam. Pulsed lasers send out a high-powered beam at regular intervals.

Aluminum

- **Aluminum** is the most common metal on the Earth's surface. It makes up 8 percent of the Earth's crust.

- **Aluminum** never occurs naturally in its pure form; it is combines with other chemicals as minerals in ore rocks.

- **The major source** of aluminum is layers of soft ore called bauxite, which is mostly aluminum hydroxide.

- **Alum powders** made from aluminum compounds were used 5,000 years ago for dyeing. Pure aluminum was first made in 1825 by Danish scientist Hans Oersted.

- **Aluminum** production was the first industrial process to use hydroelectricity when Paul Héroult set up a plant on the river Rhine in 1887.

- **Aluminum is silver** in color when freshly made, but tarnishes to white. It is slow to corrode.

- **Aluminum** is one of the

▲ Although aluminum is common in the ground, it is worth recycling because extracting it from bauxite uses a lot of energy.

◄ Half of the soft drinks cans in the U.S.A. are made from recycled aluminum.

lightest metals. It weighs just one-third as much as steel.

- **Aluminum oxide** can crystallize into one of the hardest minerals, corundum, which is used to sharpen knives.

- **Aluminum** melts at 1,200°F (650°C) and boils at 4,440 °F (2,450°C).

- **Each year 21 million tons** of aluminum are made, mostly from bauxite dug up in Brazil and New Guinea.

Stretching and pulling

▲ The leverage of the bow string helps an archer bend the bow so far that it has tremendous power as it snaps back into shape.

- **Elasticity** is the ability of a solid material to return to its original shape after it has been misshapen.

- **A force** that misshapes material is called a stress.

- **All solids** are slightly elastic but some are very elastic, for example rubber, thin steel, and young skin.

- **Solids** return to their original shape after the stress stops, if the stress is less than their "elastic limit."

- **Strain** is how much a solid is stretched or squeezed when under stress, namely how much longer it grows.

- **The amount** a solid stretches under a particular force— the ratio of stress to strain—is called the elastic modulus, or Young's modulus.

- **The greater the stress**, the greater the strain. This is called Hooke's law, after Robert Hooke (1635–1703).

- **Solids** with a low elastic modulus, like rubber, are stretchier than ones with a high modulus, such as steel.

- **Steel can be stretched** by 1 percent before it reaches its elastic limit. If the steel is coiled into a spring, this 1 percent can allow a lot of stretching and squeezing.

> ★ STAR FACT ★
> Rubber can be stretched 1,000 times beyond its original length before it reaches its elastic limit.

Electrons

- **Electrons** are by far the smallest of the three main, stable parts of every atom; the other two parts are protons and neutrons (see Atoms). In a normal atom there are the same number of electrons as protons.

- **Electrons** are 1,836 times as small as protons and have a mass of just 9.109 x 10^{-31}kg. 10^{-31} means there are 30 zeros after the decimal point. So they weigh almost nothing.

- **Electrons were discovered** by English physicist Joseph John Thomson in 1897 as he studied the glow in a cathode-ray tube (see Television). This was the first time anyone realized that the atom is not just one solid ball.

- **Electrons are** packets of energy. They can be thought of either as a tiny vibration or wave, or as a ball-like particle. They travel as waves and arrive as particles.

- **You can never be sure** just where an electron is. It is better to think of an electron circling the nucleus not as a planet circling the Sun but as a cloud wrapped around it. Electron clouds near the nucleus are round, but those farther out are other shapes, such as dumb-bells.

- **Electrons** have a negative electrical charge. This means they are attracted to positive electrical charges and repelled by negative charges. "Electron" comes from the Greek word for amber. Amber tingles electrically when rubbed.

- **Electrons cling** to the nucleus because protons have

▶ *Each atom has a different number of electrons. Its chemical character depends on the number of electrons in its outer shell. Atoms with only one electron in their outer shell, such as lithium, sodium, and potassium, have many properties in common. The electron shell structures for five common atoms are shown here.*

★ STAR FACT ★
Electrons whizz round an atomic nucleus, zoom through an electric wire or spin on their own axis, either clockwise or anti-clockwise.

a positive charge equal to the electron's negative charge.

- **Electrons have so much energy** that they move too fast to fall into the nucleus. Instead they circle the nucleus at different distances depending on how much energy they have. The more energetic an electron, the farther from the nucleus it is. There is room for only one other electron at each energy level, and it must be spinning in the opposite way. This is called Pauli's exclusion principle.

- **Electrons are** stacked around the nucleus in shells. Each shell is labeled with a letter and can hold up to a particular number of electrons. Shell K can hold up to 2, L 8, M 18, N 32, O about 50, and P about 72.

Hydrogen atom

Single electron

Nucleus with single proton

Carbon atom

Nucleus with 6 protons

Maximum 2 electrons in shell K

Shell L holds 4 electrons out of a possible 8. So carbon has four vacancies to form complex compounds with other elements

Oxygen atom

Nucleus with 8 protons

Shell K holds a maximum of 2 electrons

Shell L holds 6 electrons out of a possible 8. So oxygen has 2 "missing" electrons and is very reactive

Chlorine atom

Nucleus with 17 protons

Sodium atom

Nucleus with 11 protons

Shell L holds a maximum of 8 electrons, so the next electron goes in shell M

Single electron in shell M is easily drawn to other atoms

7 electrons out of 8 in shell M means that chlorine is drawn to atoms with a spare electron

Oxygen

▲ No animal can live for more than a minute or so without breathing in oxygen from the air to keep the body processes going.

- **Oxygen** is the second most plentiful element on Earth, making up 46 percent of the Earth's crust. Air is 20.94 percent oxygen.

- **Oxygen** is one of the most reactive elements. This is why oxygen in the Earth's crust is usually found joined with other chemicals in compounds.

- **Oxygen has an atomic number** of 8 and an atomic weight of 15.9994.

- **Oxygen molecules** in the air are made from two oxygen atoms; three oxygen atoms make the gas ozone.

- **Oxygen turns to a pale blue liquid** at 297.3°F (−182.96°C). It freezes at 218.4°F (−218.4°C).

- **Most life depends on oxygen** because it joins with other chemicals in living cells to give the energy needed for life processes. The process of using oxygen in living cells is called cellular respiration.

- **Liquid oxygen,** or LOX, is combined with fuels such as kerosene to provide rocket fuel.

- **Oxygen** was discovered independently by Carl Scheele and Joseph Priestley during the 1770s.

- **The name** "oxygen" means acid-forming. It was given to the gas in 1779 by Antoine Lavoisier (see Lavoisier).

> ★ STAR FACT ★
> The oxygen in the air on which your life depends was produced mainly by algae.

Einstein

▶ Einstein's equation $E=mc^2$ revealed the energy in atoms that led to nuclear bombs and nuclear power.

- **Albert Einstein** (1879–1955) was the most famous scientist of the 20th century.

- **Einstein was half German** and half Swiss, but when Hitler came to power in 1933, Einstein made his home in the U.S.A.

- **Einstein's fame** rests on his two theories of Relativity (see Relativity).

- **His theory of Special Relativity** was published in 1905 while he worked in the Patent Office in Bern, Switzerland.

- **In 1905** Einstein also explained the photoelectric effect. From these ideas, photo cells were developed. These are the basis of TV cameras and many other devices.

- **Einstein** completed his theory of General Relativity in 1915 while Germany was at war.

- **Einstein** was not satisfied with his theory of General Relativity because it did not include electromagnetism. He spent the last 25 years of his life trying to develop a "Unified Field Theory" to include it.

- **Einstein** was once reported to have said that only 12 people in the world could understand his theory. He denied saying it.

- **Einstein suggested** to the U.S. government that Germany was almost certainly developing an atomic weapon as WWII started. This meant that the U.S. began developing one too.

- **Einstein was married twice.** His first wife was Mileva Maric. His second wife, Elsa, was also his first cousin.

Atoms

- **Atoms are** the tiny bits, or particles, which build together to make every substance. An atom is the tiniest bit of any pure substance.

- **You could fit** two billion atoms on the period here.

- **The number of atoms** in the Universe is about 10 followed by 80 zeros.

- **Atoms are mostly** empty space dotted with a few even tinier particles called subatomic particles.

- **In the center** of each atom is a dense core, or nucleus, made from two kinds of particle: protons and neutrons. Protons have a positive electrical charge, and neutrons none. Both protons and neutrons are made from different combinations of quarks (see Quarks).

- **If an atom** were the size of a sports arena, its nucleus would be the size of a pea.

◀ Inside every atom tiny electrons (blue) whiz around a dense nucleus built up from protons (red) and neutrons (green). The numbers of each particle vary from element to element.

- **Around the nucleus** whiz even tinier, negatively-charged particles called electrons (see Electrons).

- **Atoms can be split** but they are usually held together by three forces: the electrical attraction between positive protons and negative electrons, and the strong and weak "nuclear" forces that hold the nucleus together.

- **Every element** is made from atoms with a certain number of protons in the nucleus. An iron atom has 26 protons, gold has 79. The number of protons is the atomic number.

- **Atoms with the same number** of protons but a different number of neutrons are called isotopes.

Microscopes

- **Microscopes** are devices for looking at things that are normally too small for the human eye to see.

- **Optical microscopes** use lenses to magnify the image by up to 2,000 times.

- **In an optical microscope** an objective lens bends light rays apart to enlarge what you see; an eyepiece lens makes the big image visible.

- **Electron microscopes** magnify by firing streams of electrons at the object. The electrons bounce off the object onto a fluorescent screen which makes them visible.

- **An electron microscope** can focus on something as small as 1 nanometer (one-billionth of a meter) and magnify it five million times.

- **Scanning Electron Microscopes** (SEMs) scan the surface of an object to magnify it by up to 100,000 times.

- **Transmission Electron Microscopes** shine through thin slices of an object to magnify it millions of times.

- **Scanning Tunneling Microscopes** are so powerful that they can reveal individual atoms.

- **The idea of electron microscopes** came from French physicist Louis de Broglie in 1924.

- **Scanning Acoustic Microscopes** use sound waves to see inside tiny opaque objects.

◀▼ A Scanning Electron Microscope clearly reveals the tiny nerve fibers inside the human brain.

Electromagnetic spectrum

- **The electromagnetic spectrum** is the complete range of radiation sent out by electrons (see Light and Atoms). It is given off in tiny packages of energy called photons, which can be either particles or waves (see Moving light).

- **Electromagnetic waves** vary in length and frequency. The shorter the wave, the higher its frequency (and also its energy).

- **The longest waves** are over 6omi (100km) long; the shortest are less than a billionth of an inch long.

- **All electromagnetic waves** travel at 186,411mi/sec (300,000km/sec), which is the speed of light.

- **Visible light** is just a small part of the spectrum.

- **Radio waves,** including microwaves and television waves, and infrared light, are made from waves that are too long for human eyes to see.

- **Long waves** are lower in energy than short waves. Long waves from space penetrate the Earth's atmosphere easily (but not solids, like short waves).

- **Ultraviolet light,** X-rays, and gamma rays are made from waves that are too short for human eyes to see.

- **Short waves are very energetic.** But short waves from space are blocked out by Earth's atmosphere—which is fortunate because they are dangerous. X-rays and gamma rays penetrate some solids, and UV rays can damage living tissue, causing skin cancers.

> ★ STAR FACT ★
> Cosmic rays are not rays but streams of high-energy particles from space.

Gamma rays are dangerous high-energy rays with such short waves that they can penetrate solids. They are created in space and by nuclear bombs

X-rays are longer waves than gamma rays but short enough to pass through most body tissues except bones, which show up white on medical X-ray photos

The shortest ultraviolet rays in sunshine are dangerous, but longer ones give you a suntan in small doses. In large doses even long UV rays cause cancer

Visible light varies in wavelength from violet (shortest) through all the colors of the rainbow to red (longest)

◄ This illustration shows the range of radiation in the electromagnetic spectrum. The waves are shown emerging from the Sun because the Sun actually emits almost the full range of radiation. Fortunately, the atmosphere protects us from the dangerous ones.

Infrared light is the radiation given out by hot objects. This is why infrared-sensitive "thermal imaging" cameras can see hot objects such as people in pitch darkness

Microwaves are used to beam telephone signals to satellites—and to cook food. Radars send out fairly short microwaves (about 0.3in/1cm long)

Television broadcasts use radio waves with waves about 1.5ft (0.5m) long

Radio broadcasts use radio waves with waves from 985ft (300m) to 5,000ft (1,500m) long

Typical wavelength in meters or millimeters. Long waves are low frequency and low energy. Short waves are high frequency and high energy

1 billionth mm

10 millionth mm

0.00001 mm

0.0005 mm

0.2 mm

0.3 mm to 1 mm

0.5 m

300–1,500 m

Chemical bonds

- **Chemical bonds** link together atoms to make molecules (see Molecules).

- **Atoms can bond** in three main ways: ionic bonds, covalent bonds, and metallic bonds.

- **In ionic bonds** electrons are transferred between atoms.

- **Ionic bonds** occur when atoms with just a few electrons in their outer shell give the electrons to atoms with just a few missing from their outer shell.

- **An atom** that loses an electron becomes positively charged; an atom that gains an electron becomes negatively charged so the two atoms are drawn together by the electrical attraction of opposites.

- **Sodium** loses an electron and chlorine gains one to form the ionic bond

◀ Each of the four hydrogen atoms in methane shares its electron with the central carbon atom to create strong covalent bonds.

▶ In this carbon dioxide molecule the carbon is held to two oxygen atoms by covalent bonds.

of sodium chloride (table salt) molecules.

- **In covalent bonding,** the atoms in a molecule share electrons.

- **Because they are negatively** charged, the shared electrons are drawn equally to the positive nucleus of both atoms involved. The atoms are held together by the attraction between each nucleus and the shared electrons.

- **In metallic bonds** huge numbers of atoms lose their electrons. They are held together in a lattice by the attraction between "free" electrons and positive nuclei.

> ★ STAR FACT ★
> Seven elements, including hydrogen, are found in nature only as two atoms covalently bonded.

Pressure

▶ The worst storms, such as this hurricane seen from space, are caused when air from high-pressure areas rushes into low-pressure areas

- **Pressure** is the force created by the assault of fast-moving molecules.

- **The pressure that keeps** a bicycle tire inflated is the constant assault of huge numbers of air molecules on the inside of the tire.

- **The water pressure that** crushes a submarine when it dives too deep is the assault of huge numbers of water molecules.

- **Pressure rises** as you go deeper in the ocean. This is because of an increasing weight of water—called hydrostatic pressure—pressing down from above.

- **The water pressure** 10,000m below the surface is equivalent to seven elephants standing on a dinner plate.

- **The pressure of the air** on the outside of your body is balanced by the pressure of fluids inside. Without this internal pressure, air pressure would crush your body instantly.

- **Pressure** is measured as the force on a certain area.

- **The standard unit** of pressure is a pascal (Pa) or 1 newton/sq m (N/m²).

- **High pressures:** the center of the Earth may be 400 billion Pa; steel can withstand 40 million Pa; a shark bite can be 30 million Pa.

- **Low pressures:** the best laboratory vacuum is 1 trillionth Pa; the quietest sound is 200 millionths Pa. The pressure of sunlight may be 3 millionths Pa.

Machines

- **A machine** is a device that makes doing work easier by reducing the effort needed to move something.

- **There are two forces** involved in every machine: the Load that the machine has to overcome, and the Effort used to move the Load.

- **The amount that a machine** reduces the Effort needed to move a Load is called the Mechanical Advantage. This tells you how effective a machine is.

- **Basic machines include** levers, gears, pulleys, screws, wedges, and wheels. More elaborate machines, such as cranes, are built up from combinations of these basic machines.

- **Machines cut** the effort needed to move a Load by spreading the Effort over a greater distance or time.

- **The distance** moved by the Effort you apply, divided

◄ *Like many aspects of modern life, farming has become increasingly dependent on the use of machines.*

by the distance moved by the Load, is called the Velocity Ratio (VR).

- **If the VR is greater** than 1, then the Effort moves farther than the Load. You need less effort to move the load, but you have to apply the effort for longer.

- **The total amount** of effort you use to move something is called Work. Work is the force you apply multiplied by the distance that the load moves.

- **One of the earliest machines is still used today.** It is a screw-like water-lifting device called a dalu, first used in Sumeria 5,500 years ago.

- **One of the world's biggest machines** is the SMEC earthmover used in opencast mines in Australia. It weighs 180 tons and has wheels 11.5ft (3.5m) high.

Faraday

▲ *Faraday drew huge crowds to his brilliant and entertaining Christmas lectures on science at the Royal Institution in London. These Christmas lectures at the Royal Institution continue to be a popular tradition today.*

- **Michael Faraday** (1791–1867) was one of the greatest scientists of the 19th century.

- **Faraday was the son** of a poor blacksmith, born in the village of Newington in Surrey, England.

- **He started work as** an apprentice bookbinder but became assistant to the great scientist Humphry Davy after taking brilliant notes at one of Davy's lectures.

- **Faraday was said** to be Davy's greatest discovery.

- **Until 1830 Faraday** was mainly a chemist. In 1825, he discovered the important chemical benzene.

- **In 1821** Faraday showed that the magnetism created by an electric current would make a magnet move and so a very simple version of an electric motor.

- **In 1831** Faraday showed that when a magnet moves close to an electric wire, it creates, or induces, an electric current in the wire. This was discovered at the same time by Joseph Henry in the U.S.A.

- **Using** his discovery of electric induction, Faraday made the first dynamo to generate electricity and so opened the way to the modern age of electricity.

- **In the 1840s** Faraday suggested the idea of lines of magnetic force and electromagnetic fields. These ideas, which were later developed by James Clerk Maxwell, underpin much of modern science.

- **Faraday** was probably the greatest scientific experimenter of all time.

Electric circuits

- **An electric charge** that does not move is called static electricity (see Electricity). A charge may flow in a current providing there is an unbroken loop, or circuit.

- **A current only flows** through a good conductor such as copper, namely a material that transmits charge well.

- **A current only flows** if there is a driving force to push the charge. This force is called an electromotive force (emf).

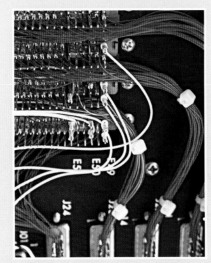

- **The emf** is created by a battery or a generator.

▶ *For a current to flow, each of these wires must form a circuit.*

- **Currents were once thought to** flow like water. In fact they move like a row of marbles bumping into each other.

- **In a good conductor** there are lots of free electrons that are unattached to atoms. These are the "marbles."

- **A current only flows** if there are more electrons at one point in the circuit. This difference, called the potential difference, is measured in volts.

- **The rate at which current** flows is measured in amps. It depends on the voltage and the resistance (how much the circuit obstructs the flow of current). Resistance is measured in ohms.

- **Batteries** give out Direct Current, a current that flows in one direction. Power stations send out Alternating Current , which swaps direction 50–60 times per second.

Plastics

- **Plastics are synthetic** (man-made) materials that can be easily shaped and molded.

- **Most plastics are polymers** (see New materials). The structure of polymer molecules gives plastic different properties.

- **Long chains of molecules** that slide over each other easily make flexible plastics such as polythene. Tangled chains make rigid plastics such as melamine.

- **Typically** plastics are made by joining carbon and hydrogen atoms. These form ethene molecules, which can be joined to make a plastic called polythene.

- **Many plastics** are made from liquids and gases that are extracted from crude oil.

- **Thermoplastics** are soft and easily molded when warm but set solid when cool. They are used to make bottles and drainpipes and can be melted again.

- **Thermoset plastics,** which cannot be remelted once set, are used to make telephones and pan handles.

- **Blow molding** involves using compressed air to push a tube of plastic into a mold.

- **Vacuum molding** involves using a vacuum to suck a sheet of plastic into a mold.

- **Extrusion molding** involves heating plastic pellets and forcing them out through a nozzle to give the right shape.

▼ *Some plastics are light and soft and can be filled with air bubbles to make an ideal packing material.*

Chemical compounds

- **Compounds** are substances that are made when the atoms of two or more different elements join together.

- **The properties of a compound** are usually very different from those of the elements which it is made of.

- **Compounds** are different from mixtures because the elements are joined together chemically. They can only be separated by a chemical reaction.

- **Every molecule** of a compound is exactly the same combination of atoms.

- **The scientific name** of a compound is usually a combination of the elements involved, although it might have a different common name.

- **Table salt** is the chemical compound sodium chloride. Each molecule has one sodium and one chlorine atom.

- **The chemical formula** of a compound summarizes which atoms a molecule is made of. The chemical formula for water is H_2O because each water molecule has two hydrogen (H) atoms and one oxygen (O) atom.

- **There only 100 or so elements** but they can combine in different ways to form many millions of compounds.

- **The same combination of elements,** such as carbon and hydrogen, can form many different compounds.

- **Compounds** are either organic (see Organic chemistry), which means they contain carbon atoms, or inorganic.

▼ *The molecules of a compound are identical combinations of atoms.*

Halogens

▲ *Chlorine is often added to the water in swimming pools to kill bacteria, giving the water a greenish-blue tinge.*

- **Halogens** are the chemical elements fluorine, chlorine, bromine, iodine, and astatine.

- **The word "halogen"** means salt-forming. All halogens easily form salt compounds.

- **Many of the salts in the sea** are compounds of a halogen and a metal, such as sodium chloride and magnesium chloride.

- **The halogens** all have a strong, often nasty, smell.

- **Fluorine** is a pale yellow gas, chlorine a greenish gas, bromine a red liquid, and iodine a black solid.

- **Astatine** is an unstable element that survives by itself only briefly. It is usually made artificially.

- **The halogens** together form Group 7 of the Periodic Table, elements with seven electrons in the outer shells.

- **Because halogens have** one electron missing, they form negative ions and are highly reactive.

- **The iodine and bromine** in a halogen lightbulb make it burn brighter and longer.

★ **STAR FACT** ★
Fluorides (fluorine compounds) are often added to drinking water to prevent tooth decay.

Particle physics

- **Apart from the three** basic, stable particles of atoms: electrons, protons, and neutrons, scientists have found over 200 rare or short-lived particles. Some were found in cosmic rays from space; some appear when atoms are smashed to bits in devices called particle accelerators.

- **Every particle** also has a mirror-image anti-particle. Although Antimatter is much rarer, it is every bit as real.

- **Cosmic rays** contain not only electrons, protons, and neutrons, but short-lived particles such as muons and strange quarks. Muons flash into existence for 2.2 microseconds just before the cosmic rays reach the ground.

- **Smashing atoms** in particle accelerators creates short-lived high-energy particles such as taus and pions and three kinds of quark called charm, bottom, and top.

- **Particles** are now grouped into a simple framework called the Standard Model. It divides them into elementary particles and composite particles to stop radiation leaks.

- **Elementary particles** are the basic particles which cannot be broken down in anything smaller. There are three groups: quarks, leptons, and bosons. Leptons include electrons, muons, taus, and neutrinos. Bosons are "messenger" particles that link the others. They include photons and gluons which "glue" quarks together.

- **Composite particles** are hadrons made of quarks glued together by gluons. They include protons, neutrons, and "hyperons" and "resonances."

- **To smash atoms** scientists use particle accelerators, which are giant machines set in tunnels. The accelerators use powerful magnets to accelerate particles through a tube at huge speeds, and then smash them together.

- **Huge detectors** pick up collisions between particles.

▼ *A view of the particle accelerator tunnel at CERN in Switzerland.*

Incredibly powerful electromagnets accelerate the particles

Extra electromagnets keep the particles on track through the pipe

The particles are split up and fed towards the detector from opposite directions so they collide head-on

Some accelerators are ring-shaped so that the particles can whiz around again and again to build up speed

New particles are fed in from a hot filament like a giant lightbulb filament

The detectors that record the collisions are like giant electronic cameras. They can be three stories high and weigh over 5,000 tons

The pipes are heavily insulated to stop particles from escaping

◄ *The accelerators at Fermilab near Chicago, USA and CERN in Switzerland are underground tubes many miles long through which particles are accelerated to near the speed of light.*

Forces

- **A force** is a push or a pull. It can make something start to move, slow down or speed up, change direction, or change shape or size. The greater a force, the more effect it has.

- **The wind is a force.** Biting, twisting, stretching, lifting, and many other actions are also forces. Every time something happens, a force is involved.

- **Force is measured** in newtons (N). One newton is the force needed to speed up a mass of one kilogram by one meter per second every second.

- **When something moves** there are usually several forces involved. When you throw a ball, the force of your throw hurls it forward, the force of gravity pulls it down, and the force of air resistance slows it down.

> ★ STAR FACT ★
> The thrust of *Saturn V*'s rocket engines was 33 million newtons.

- **The direction and speed** of movement depend on the combined effect of all the forces involved—this is called the resultant.

- **A force** has magnitude (size) and works in a particular direction.

- **A force can** be drawn on a diagram as an arrow called a vector (see Vectors). The arrow's direction shows the force's direction. Its length shows the force's strength.

- **Four fundamental forces** operate throughout the Universe: gravity, electric and magnetic forces (together called electromagnetic force), and strong and weak nuclear forces (see Nuclear energy).

- **A force field** is the area over which a force has an effect. The field is strongest closest to the source and gets weaker farther away.

◀ When a spacecraft lifts off, the force of the rocket has to overcome the forces of gravity and air resistance to power it upward.

Electricity

- **Electricity** is the energy that makes everything from toasters to televisions work. It is also linked to magnetism. Together, as electromagnetism, they are one of the fundamental forces holding the Universe together.

- **Electricity** is made by tiny bits of atoms called electrons. Electrons have an electrical charge which is a force that either pulls bits of atoms together or pushes them apart.

▼ Lightning is probably the most dramatic display of electricity.

- **Some particles** (bit of atoms) have a negative electrical charge; others have a positive charge.

- **Particles** with the same charge push each other away. Particles with the opposite charge pull together.

- **Electrons** have a negative electrical charge.

- **There are the same number** of positive and negative particles in most atoms so the charges usually balance out.

- **Electricity** is created when electrons move, building up negative charge in one place or carrying it along.

- **Static electricity** is when the negative charge stays in one place. Current electricity is when the charge moves.

- **Electric charge** is measured with an electroscope.

- **Materials** that let electrons (and electrical charge) move through them easily, such as copper, are called conductors. Materials that stop electrons passing through, such as rubber, are called insulators.

Time

▲ As the Sun moves through the sky we can clearly see the passing of time. Until 1967 the movement of the Sun was our most accurate way of measuring time.

- **No clock** keeps perfect time. Mostly, clocks were set by the Sun and stars.
- **Since 1967** the world's time has been set by atomic clocks.
- **Atomic clocks** are accurate to 0.001 sec in 1,000 years.
- **If a cesium atomic** clock ran for six million years it would not gain or lose a second.
- **The world's most** accurate clock is the American NIST-7 atomic clock.
- **The atomic clock** on the International Space Station is hundreds of times more accurate than clocks on Earth, because it is not affected by gravity.
- **Atomic clocks** work because cesium atoms vibrate exactly 9,192,631,770 times a second.
- **Some scientists** say that time is the fourth dimension—the other three are length, breadth, and height. So time could theoretically run in any direction. Others say time only moves in one direction. (see Time travel).
- **Light takes** millions of years to reach us from distant galaxies, so we see them not as they are but as they were millions of years ago. Light takes a little while to reach us even from nearby things. So time depends on where you measure it (see Relativity).
- **Einstein's theory of General Relativity** shows that time actually runs slower nearer strong gravitational fields such as stars. This does not mean that the clock is running slower but that time itself is running slower.

Chemical reactions

- **A candle burning,** a nail rusting, a cake cooking—all involve chemical reactions.
- **A chemical reaction** is when two or more elements or compounds meet and interact to form new compounds or separate out some of the elements.
- **The chemicals** involved in a chemical reaction are called the reactants. The results are called the products.
- **The products** contain exactly the same atoms as the reactants but in different combinations.
- **The products** have exactly the same total mass as the reactants. This is called conservation of mass.
- **Some reactions** are reversible, which means the products can be changed back to the original reactants. Others, such as making toast, are irreversible.
- **Effervescence** is a reaction in which gas bubbles form in a liquid, turning it fizzy.
- **A catalyst** is a substance that speeds up or enables a chemical reaction to happen, but is not involved itself.
- **Nearly all reactions** involve energy. Some involve light or electricity. Most involve heat. Reactions that give out heat are called exothermic. Those that draw in heat are called endothermic.
- **Oxidation** is a reaction in which oxygen combines with a substance. Burning is oxidation; as the fuel burns it combines with oxygen in the air. Reduction is a reaction in which a substance loses oxygen.

▶ Burning is an oxidation reaction. Carbon in the trees combines with oxygen in the air to form carbon dioxide.

The Periodic Table

- **The Periodic Table** is a chart of all the 100–plus or so different chemical elements (see Elements).

- **The Periodic Table** was devised by Russian chemist Dmitri Mendeleyev (1834–1907) in 1869. Mendeleyev realized that each element is part of a complete set, and so he predicted the existence of three then unknown elements—gallium, scandium, and germanium.

- **The Periodic Table** arranges all the elements according to their Atomic Number, which is the number of protons in their atoms (see Atoms). The table lists the elements in order of Atomic Number, starting with hydrogen at 1.

- **Atoms** usually have the same number of electrons (see Electrons) as protons. So the Atomic Number also indicates the normal number of electrons an atom has.

- **Atomic mass** is the average weight of an atom of an element and corresponds to the average number of protons and neutrons in the nucleus. The number of neutrons varies in a small number of atoms, called isotopes, so the atomic mass is never a round number.

- **The columns** in the Periodic Table are called Groups. The rows are called Periods.

- **The number** of layers, or shells, of electrons in the atoms of an element increases one by one down each Group. So all the elements in each Period have the same number of electron shells.

- **The number of electrons** in the atom's outer shell goes up one by one across each Period.

- **Each Group** is made up of elements with a certain number of electrons in their outer shell. This is what largely determines the element's character. All the elements in each Group have similar properties. Many of the Groups have a name as well as a number.

- **Each Period** starts on the left with a highly reactive alkali metal of Group 1, such as sodium. Each atom of elements in Group 1 has a single electron in its outer shell. Each period ends on the right with a stable "noble" gas of Group 18, such as argon. These elements have the full number of electrons in their outer shell and do not react.

Above the name for each element is its abbreviation, or "formula"

Below the name for each element is the Atomic Number

As Atomic Numbers increase by one along each period, so chemical properties change

These elements (sand-colored) are called non-metals

These elements (green) are called poor metals

The final group (group 18) on the right is the noble gases

Group 1 is called alkali metals. They are all soft, very reactive metals

Group 2 is the alkaline–earth group. They occur naturally only in compounds

The block in the middle (purple) is transition metals such as gold and copper

This row, called the lanthanides, or rare earths, fits into Group 13. All are shiny metals

This row, called the actinides, fits into Group 13. It includes radium and plutonium

▲ There are eight columns or Groups across in the Periodic Table and seven rows or Periods down. The block of transition metals in the middle fits into Group 13. Each element has three electrons in its outer shell, but different numbers in the inner shells.

Crystals

- **Crystals** are particular kinds of solids that are made from a regular arrangement, or lattice, of atoms. Most rocks and metals are crystals, so are snowflakes and salt.

- **Most crystals** have regular, geometrical shapes with smooth faces and sharp corners.

- **Most crystals** grow in dense masses, as in metals. Some crystals grow separately, like grains of sugar.

- **Some crystals** are shiny and clear to look at. Crystals got their name from the chunks of quartz that the ancient Greeks called *krystallos*. They believed the chunks were unmeltable ice.

- **Crystals** form by a process called crystallization. As liquid evaporates or molten solids cool, the chemicals dissolved in them solidify.

▶ *Crystals such as these grow naturally as minerals are deposited from hot mineral-rich liquids underground.*

- **Crystals** grow gradually as more and more atoms attach themselves to the lattice, just as icicles grow as water freezes onto them.

- **The smallest crystals** are microscopically small. Occasionally crystals of a mineral such as beryl may grow to the size of telegraph poles.

- **A liquid crystal** is a crystal that can flow like a liquid but has a regular pattern of atoms.

- **A liquid crystal** may change color or go dark when the alignment of its atoms is disrupted by electricity or heat. Liquid crystal displays (LCDs) use a tiny electric current to make crystals affect light.

- **X-ray crystallography** uses X-rays to study the structure of atoms in a crystal. This is how we know the structure of many important life substances.

Friction

- **Friction** is the force that acts between two things rubbing together. It stops them from sliding past each other.

- **The friction** that stops things starting to slide is called static friction. The friction that slows down sliding surfaces is called dynamic friction.

- **The harder** two surfaces are pressed together, the greater the force that is needed to overcome friction.

- **The coefficient of friction (CF)** is the ratio of the friction to the weight of the sliding object.

- **Metal sliding on metal** has a CF of 0.74; ice sliding on ice has a CF of 0.1. This means it is over seven times harder to make metal slide on metal than ice on ice.

- **Friction often makes things hot**. As the sliding object is slowed down, much of the energy of its momentum is turned into heat.

- **Fluid friction** is the friction between moving fluids or between a fluid and a solid. It is what makes thick fluids viscous (less runny).

- **Oil reduces friction** by creating a film that keeps the solid surfaces apart.

- **Brakes use dynamic friction** to slow things down.

- **Drag is friction** between air and an object. It slows a fast car, or any aircraft moving through the air.

▼ *Waxed skis on snow have a CF of just 0.14, allowing cross-country skiers to slide along the ground very easily.*

Lavoisier

- **Antoine Laurent Lavoisier** (1743–1794) was a brilliant French scientist who is regarded as the founder of modern chemistry.

- **He was elected** to the French Royal Academy of Sciences at just 25 for an essay on street lighting. A year later, he worked on the first geological map of France.

- **Lavoisier earned his living** for a long while as a "tax farmer," which meant he worked for a private company collecting taxes.

- **In 1771** he married 14-year-old Marie Paulze, who later became his illustrator and collaborator in the laboratory.

- **Lavoisier** was the first person to realize that air is essentially a mixture of two gases: oxygen and nitrogen.

- **Lavoisier discovered** that water is a compound of hydrogen and oxygen.

◄ *Lavoisier showed the importance of precision weighing in the laboratory.*

- **Lavoisier** showed that the popular phlogiston theory of burning was wrong and that burning involves oxygen instead.

- **Lavoisier** gave the first working list of chemical elements in his famous book *Elementary Treatise of Chemistry* (1789), which was illustrated by his wife Marie.

- **From 1776** Lavoisier headed research at the Royal Arsenal in Paris, developing gunpowder manufacture.

- **Lavoisier ran schemes** for public education, fair taxation, old-age insurance, and other welfare schemes. But his good deeds did not save him. When Lavoisier had a wall built round Paris to reduce smuggling, revolutionary leader Marat accused him of imprisoning Paris's air. His past as a tax farmer was remembered and Lavoisier was guillotined in 1794.

Electromagnetism

▲ *Wind turbines generate electricity by using the wind to turn their blades. These drive magnets around inside coils of electric wire.*

- **Electromagnetism** is the combined effect of electricity and magnetism.

- **Every electric current** creates its own magnetic field.

- **Maxwell's screw rule** says that the magnetic field runs the same way a screw turns if you screw it in the direction of the electric current.

- **An electromagnet** is a strong magnet that is only magnetic when an electric current passes through it. It is made by wrapping a coil of wire, called a solenoid, around a core of iron.

- **Electromagnets** are used in everything from ticket machines and telephones to loudspeakers.

- **Magnetic levitation** trains use strong electromagnets to carry the train on a cushion of magnetic repulsion.

- **When an electric wire** is moved across a magnetic field, an electric current is created, or induced, in the wire. This is the basis of every kind of electricity generation.

- **Fleming's right-hand rule** says that if you hold your right thumb, first and middle fingers at 90° to each other, your middle finger shows the direction of the induced current—if your thumb points in the direction the wire moves and your first finger points out the magnetic field.

- **Electromagnetism** is one of the fundamental forces of the Universe. It holds electrons onto atoms.

- **Around every** electric or magnetic object is an area, or electromagnetic field, where its force is effective.

Heat

- **Heat is the energy** of moving molecules. The faster molecules move, the hotter it is.
- **When you hold your hand** over a heater the warmth is the assault of billions of fast-moving molecules of air.
- **Heat** is the combined energy of all the moving molecules; temperature is how fast they are moving.
- **The coldest temperature possible** is absolute zero, or 459.6°F (−273°C), when molecules stop moving.
- **When you heat a substance** its temperature rises because heat makes its molecules move faster.
- **The same amount** of heat raises the temperature of different substances by different amounts.
- **Specific heat** is the energy needed, in joules, to heat a substance by 33.8°F (1°C).

> ★ **STAR FACT** ★
> Heat makes the molecules of a solid vibrate;
> it makes gas molecules zoom around.

- **Argon gas** gets hotter quicker than oxygen. The shape of oxygen molecules means they absorb some energy not by moving faster but by spinning faster.
- **Heat always spreads out** from its source. It heats up its surroundings while cooling down itself.

◀ Fire changes the energy in fuel into heat energy. Heat makes the molecules rush around.

Iron and steel

- **Iron** is the most common element in the world. It makes up 35 percent of the Earth, but most of it is in the core.
- **Iron is never found** in its pure form in the Earth's crust. Instead it is found in iron ores, which must be heated in a blast furnace to extract the iron.
- **The chemical symbol** for iron is Fe from *ferrum*, the Latin word for iron. Iron compounds are called either ferrous or ferric.
- **Iron has** an atomic number of 26 and an atomic weight of 55.85.

◀ A solid-state laser can cut through carbon steel like butter although steel is incredibly tough.

- **Iron melts** at 2,795°F (1,535°C) and boils at 5,432°F (3,000°C). It conducts heat and electricity, dissolves slowly in water, and is easily magnetized. It loses its magnetism easily but steel can be permanently magnetic.
- **Iron** combines easily with oxygen to form iron oxide, especially in the presence of moisture. This is rusting.
- **Cast iron** is iron with 2–4 percent carbon and 1–3 percent silicon. It is suitable for pouring into sand molds. Wrought iron is almost pure iron with carbon removed to make it easy to bend and shape for railings and gates.
- **Iron is made into steel** by adding traces of carbon for making cars, railroad tracks, knives, and much more. Alloy steels are made by adding traces of metals such as tungsten (for tools) and chromium (for ball bearings).
- **60 percent of steel** is made by the basic process in which oxygen is blasted over molten iron to burn out impurities.
- **Special alloy steels** such as chromium steels can be made from scrap iron (which is low in impurities) in an electric arc furnace.

Fiber optics

- **Fiber optic cables** are bundles of transparent glass threads that transmit messages by light.

- **The light is transmitted** in coded pulses.

- **A thin layer of glass,** called cladding, surrounds each fiber and stops light from escaping.

- **The cladding** reflects all the light back into the fiber so that it bends round with the fiber. This is called total internal reflection.

- **Single-mode fibers** are very narrow and the light bounces very little from side to side. These fibers are suitable for long-distance transmissions.

- **Aiming light** into the narrow core of a single-mode fiber needs the precision of a laser beam.

- **Multi-mode fibers** are wider than single-mode fibers. They accept LED (light-emitting diodes) light, so they are cheaper but they are unsuitable for long distances.

- **The largest cables** can carry hundreds of thousands of phone calls or hundreds of television channels.

▲ *A bundle of optical fibers glows with transmitted light.*

- **Underwater fiber optic cables** transmit signals under the Atlantic and Pacific Oceans.

- **Optical fibers** have medical uses, such as in endoscopes. These are flexible tubes, with a lens on the end, that are inserted into the body to look inside it. Optical fibers are used to measure blood temperature and pressure.

Metals

▼ *Metals are very tough but can be easily shaped. They are used for an enormous variety of things, from chains to cars.*

- **75 percent** of all known elements are metals.

- **Metals** ring when hit. A metal is hard but malleable, which means it can be hammered into thin sheets.

- **Metals** are usually shiny. They conduct both heat and electricity very well.

- **Metals** do not form separate molecules. Instead atoms of metal knit together with metallic bonds (see Chemical bonds) to form lattice structures.

- **The electron shells of all metals** are less than half-full. In a chemical reaction metals give up their electrons to a non-metal.

- **Most metals** occur naturally in the ground only in rocks called ores.

- **Gold, copper,** mercury, platinum, silver, and a few other rare metals occur naturally in their pure form.

- **Mercury** is the only metal that is liquid at normal temperatures. It melts at −37.97°F (−38.87°C).

- **A few atoms** of the new metal ununquadium (atomic number 114) were made in January 1999.

> ★ STAR FACT ★
> At 6,170°F (3,410°C), tungsten has the highest melting point of any metal.

Radioactivity

- **Radioactivity** is when a certain kind of atom disintegrates spontaneously and sends out little bursts of radiation from its nucleus (center).

- **Isotopes** are slightly different versions of an atom, with either more or fewer neutrons (see Atoms). With stable elements, such as carbon, only certain isotopes called radio-isotopes are radioactive.

- **Some large atoms**, such as radium and uranium, are so unstable that all their isotopes are radio-isotopes.

- **Radioactive isotopes** emit three kinds of radiation: alpha, beta, and gamma rays.

- **When the nucleus** of an atom emits alpha or beta rays it changes and becomes the atom of a different element. This is called radioactive decay.

- **Alpha rays** are streams of alpha particles. These are made from two protons and two neutrons – basically the nucleus of a helium atom. They travel only about an inch and can be stopped by a sheet of paper.

- **Beta rays** are beta particles. Beta particles are electrons (or their opposite, positrons) emitted as a neutron decays into a proton. They can travel up to 1y and can penetrate aluminum foil.

▶ The radioisotope carbon-14 is present in all living things, but when they die it begins to steadily decay radioactively. By measuring how much carbon-14 is left relative to carbon-12 isotopes, which don't decay, scientists can tell exactly when a living thing died, including wood and bone.

- **Gamma rays** are an energetic, short-wave form of electromagnetic radiation (see Electromagnetic spectrum). They are capable of penetrating most materials except lead.

- **The half-life** of a radioactive substance is the time it takes for its radioactivity to drop by half. This is much easier to assess than the time for the radioactivity to disappear altogether.

Original proportion of uranium-235

Original proportion of lead

Alpha particle

Beta particle

Thorium-231

Radium-227

Radon-223

Polonium-219

Lead-207

◀ When some rocks formed they contained the isotope uranium-235. This decays radioactively over millions of years into lead-207. The decay happens at such a steady pace that scientists can tell the rock's exact age from the proportion of uranium-235 left compared to lead-207. The higher proportion of lead-207, the older the rock.

Light and atoms

- **All light comes** from atoms. They give out light when they gain energy—by absorbing light or when hit by other particles.

- **Atoms** are normally in a "ground" state. Their electrons circle close to the nucleus where their energy is at its lowest ebb.

- **An atom emits light** when "excited" by taking in energy. Excitement boosts an electron's energy so it jumps further out from the nucleus.

- **An atom** only stays excited a fraction of second before the electron drops back in toward the nucleus.

- **As the electron** drops back inward, it lets go of the energy it gained as a tiny packet of electromagnetic radiation called a photon.

- **Electrons** do not drop in steadily like a ball rolling down a hill, but in steps, like a ball bouncing down stairs.

◀ *Spectroscopy is used to analyse the color of light from distant stars and galaxies. It allows scientists to identify what the stars are made of.*

- **Since each step** the electron drops in has a particular energy level, so the energy of the photon depends precisely on how big the steps are. Big steps send out higher-energy short-wave photons like X-rays.

- **The color of light** an atom sends out depends on the size of the steps its electrons jump down.

- **Each kind of atom** has its own range of electron energy steps, so each sends out particular colors of light. The range of colors each kind of atom sends out is called its emission spectrum. For gases, this acts like a color signature to identify in a process called spectroscopy.

- **Just as an atom** only emits certain colors, so it can only absorb certain colors. This is its absorption spectrum.

Quantum physics

Large quantum of heat emitted

Small quantum of heat emitted

Large electron jump

Small electron jump

Electron energy levels

▲ *Quantum physics shows how radiation from a hot object is emitted in little chunks called quanta.*

- **By the 1890s** most scientists thought light moves in waves.

- **Max Planck** (1858–1847) realized that the range of radiation given out by a hot object is not quite what scientists would calculate it to be if radiation is waves.

- **Planck realized** that the radiation from a hot object could be explained if the radiation came in chunks, or quanta.

- **Quanta** are very, very small. When lots of quanta are

emitted together they appear to be like smooth waves.

- **In 1905** Einstein showed that quanta explain the photo-electric effect.

- **In 1913** Niels Bohr showed how the arrangement of electrons in energy levels around an atom (see Electrons) could be thought of in a quantum way too.

- **In the 1920s** Erwin Schrödinger and Werner Heisenberg developed Bohr's idea into quantum physics, a new branch of physics for particles on the scale of atoms.

- **Quantum physics** explains how electrons emit radiation (see above). It shows that an electron is both a particle and a wave, depending on how you look at it. It seems to work for all four fundamental forces (see Forces) except gravity.

- **The development** of the technologies that gave us lasers and transistors came from quantum physics.

- **Quantum physics** predicts some strange things on the scale of atoms, such as particles appearing from nowhere and electrons seeming to know where each other are.

Floating and sinking

- **Things float** because they are less dense than water than they do in air, which is why you can lift quite a heavy person in a swimming pool. This loss of weight is called buoyancy.

- **Buoyancy** is created by the upward push, or upthrust, of the water.

- **When an object** is immersed in water, its weight pushes it down. At the same time the water pushes it

▼ The liner Titanic was said to be unsinkable. However, as soon as an iceberg breached her hull and let in water to replace the air, she sank like a stone.

back up with a force equal to the weight of water displaced (pushed out of the way). This is called Archimedes' principle (see Archimedes).

- **An object sinks** until its weight is exactly equal to the upthrust of the water, at which point it floats.

- **Things that are less dense** than water float; those that are more dense sink.

- **Steel ships** float because although steel is denser than water, their hulls are full of air. They sink until enough water is displaced to match the weight of steel and air in the hull.

- **Oil floats** on water because it is less dense.

- **Ships float** at different heights according to how heavily laden they are and how dense the water is.

- **Ships float higher** in seawater than in fresh water because salt makes the seawater denser.

- **Ships float higher** in dense cold seas than in warm tropical ones. They float higher in the winter months.

Electronics

- **Electronics** are the basis of many modern technologies, from hi-fi systems to missile control systems.

- **Electronics** are systems that control things by automatically switching tiny electrical circuits on and off.

- **Transistors** are electronic switches. They are made of materials called semiconductors that change their ability to conduct electricity.

- **Electronic systems work** by linking many transistors together so that each controls the way the others work.

- **Diodes** are transistors with two connectors. They control an electric current by switching it on or off.

- **Triodes** are transistors with three connectors that amplify the electric current (make it bigger) or reduce it.

- **A silicon chip** is thousands of transistors linked together

> ★ STAR FACT ★
> Some microprocessors can now handle billions of bits of data every second.

▲ Microprocessors contain millions of transistors in a package that is no bigger than a human fingernail.

by thin metal strips in an integrated circuit on a single crystal of silicon.

- **The electronic areas** of a chip are those treated with traces of chemicals such as boron and phosphorus, which alter the conductivity of silicon.

- **Microprocessors** are complete Central Processing Units (see Computers) on a single silicon chip.

Telecommunications

- **Telecommunications** is the almost instantaneous transmission of sounds, words, pictures, data, and information by electronic means.

- **Every communication system** needs three things: a transmitter, a communications link, and a receiver.

- **Transmitters** can be telephones or computers with modems (see The internet). They change the words, pictures, data, or sounds into an electrical signal and send it. Similar receivers pick up the signal and change it back into the right form.

- **Communications links** carry the signal from the transmitter to the receiver in two main ways. Some give a direct link through telephone lines and other cables. Some are carried on radio waves through the air, via satellite, or microwave links.

- **Telephone lines** used to be mainly electric cables which carried the signal as pulses of electricity. More and more are now fiber optics (see Fiber optics) which carry the signal as coded pulses of light.

▼ This illustration shows some of the many ways in which telecommunications are carried. At present, TV, radio, and phone links are all carried separately, but increasingly they will all be carried the same way. They will be split up only when they arrive at their destination.

- **Communications satellites** are satellites orbiting the Earth in space. Telephone calls are beamed up on radio waves to the satellite, which beams them back down to the right part of the world.

- **Microwave links** use very short radio waves to transmit telephone and other signals from one dish to another in a straight line across Earth's surface.

- **Mobile phones** or cellular phones transmit and receive phone calls directly via radio waves. The calls are picked up and sent on from a local antenna.

- **The information superhighway** is the network of high-speed links that might be achieved by combining telephone systems, cable TV and computer networks. TV programs, movies, data, direct video links, and the Internet could all enter the home in this way.

> ★ STAR FACT ★
> Calls across the ocean go one way by satellite and the other by undersea cable to avoid delays.

More and more communications are beamed off satellites in space

Signals from individual transmitters are sent on from a telephone exchange or a service provider

Computer data are translated by a modem into signals that can be carried on phone lines

Communications that travel via satellites are beamed up from antenna dishes on the ground

Telephones can link in to the phone network by a direct cable link. Mobile phones link through the air to local relay towers by radio waves

TV and radio signals are either broadcast as pulses of radio waves, sent direct via cables or bounced off satellites

Splitting the atom

▶ You cannot actually see sub-atomic particles, but after collisions they leave tracks behind them, like these particle tracks in smoke. Photographs of these tracks tell scientists a great deal.

- **In the 1890s** scientists thought that atoms were solid like billiard balls and completely unbreakable.

- **In 1897** J.J. Thomson discovered that atoms contained even smaller particles, which he called electrons (see Electrons).

- **In 1900** scientists thought atoms were like cinnamon buns with electrons like raisins on the outside.

- **In 1909** Ernest Rutherford was firing alpha particles (see Radioactivity) at a sheet of gold foil. Most went straight through, but 1 in 8,000 particles bounced back!

- **Rutherford concluded** that the atom was mostly empty space (which the alpha particles passed straight through) but had a tiny, dense nucleus at its center.

- **In 1919** Rutherford split the nucleus of a nitrogen atom with alpha particles. Small atoms could be split.

- **In 1932** James Chadwick found the nucleus contained two kinds of particle: protons and neutrons.

- **In 1933** Italian Enrico Fermi bombarded the big atoms of uranium with neutrons. Fermi thought the new atoms that formed had simply gained the neutrons.

- **In 1939** German scientists Hahn and Strassman repeated Fermi's experiment and found smaller atoms of barium.

- **Austrian Lise Meitner** realized that Hahn and Strassman had split the atom. This discovery opened the way to releasing nuclear energy by fission (see Nuclear energy).

Heat movement

- **Heat moves** in three different ways: conduction, convection, and radiation.

- **Conduction** involves heat spreading from hot areas to cold areas by direct contact. It works a bit like a relay race. Energetic, rapidly moving or vibrating molecules crash into their neighbors and start them moving.

- **Good conducting materials** such as metals feel cool to the touch because they carry heat away from your fingers quickly. The best conductors of heat are the metals silver, copper, and gold, in that order.

- **Materials** that conduct heat slowly are called insulators. They help keep things warm by reducing heat loss. Wood is one of the best insulators. Water is also surprisingly effective as an insulator, which is why some divers and surfers often wear wetsuits.

- **Radiation** is the spread of heat as heat rays, that is, invisible waves of infrared radiation.

◀ Hot air balloons work because hot air is lighter and rises through cold air.

- **Radiation** spreads heat without direct contact.

- **Convection** is when warm air rises through cool air, like a hot-air balloon.

- **Warm air rises** because warmth makes the air expand. As it expands the air becomes less dense and lighter than the cool air around it.

- **Convection currents** are circulation patterns set up as warm air (or a liquid) rises. Around the column of rising warmth, cool air continually sinks to replace it at the bottom. So the whole air turns over like a non-stop fountain.

★ STAR FACT ★
Convection currents in the air bring rain; convection currents in the Earth's interior move continents.

Light sources

▲ *Gas mixtures in neon lights glow different colors. Pure neon glows red.*

◀ *Electrical resistance makes the thin filament in a bulb glow.*

- **The light falling** on a surface is measured in lux. 1 lux is how brightly lit something is by a light of 1 candela 1m away. You need 500 lux to read by.

- **Our main sources of natural light** are the Sun and the stars. The hot gases on their surface glow fiercely.

- **The brightness** of a light source is measured in candelas (cd); 1 candela is about as bright as a small candle.

- **For 0.1 millisecond** an atom bomb flashes out 2,000 billion candelas for every square meter (m^2).

- **The Sun's surface** pumps out 23 billion candela per m^2. Laser lights are even brighter, but very small.

- **Electric lightbulbs** are incandescent, which means that their light comes from a thin tungsten wire, or filament, that glows when heated by an electric current.

- **Lightbulbs** are filled with an inert (unreactive) gas, such as argon, to save the filament from burning out.

- **Electric lights** were invented independently in 1878 by Englishman Sir Joseph Swan and Americans Thomas Alva Edison and Hiram Maxim.

- **Fluorescent lights** have a glass tube coated on the inside with powders called phosphors. When electricity excites the gases in the tube to send out invisible UV rays, the rays hit the phosphors and make them glow, or fluoresce.

- **In neon lights,** a huge electric current makes the gas inside a tube electrically charged and so it glows.

Weight and mass

- **Mass** is the amount of matter in an object.

- **Weight** is not the same as mass. Scientists say weight is the force of gravity pulling on an object. Weight varies with the mass of the object and the strength of gravity.

- **Objects weigh more** at sea level, which is nearer the center of the Earth, than up a mountain.

- **A person on the Moon** weighs one sixth of their weight on Earth because the Moon's gravity is one sixth of the Earth's gravity.

- **Weight varies** with gravity but mass is always the same, so scientists use mass when talking about how heavy something is.

▶ *Brass weights such as this one remain the standard in a chemical laboratory.*

- **The smallest** known mass is that of a photon (see Light and atoms). Its mass is 5.3 times 10^{-63} (62 zeros and a 1 after the decimal point) kg.

- **The mass of the Earth** is 6×10^{24} (six trillion trillion) kg. The mass of the Universe may be 10^{51} (10 followed by 50 zeros) kg.

- **Density is** the amount of mass in a certain space. It is measured in grams per cubic centimeter (g/cm^3).

- **The lightest** solids are silica aerogels made for space science, with a density of 0.005 g/cm^3. The lightest gas is hydrogen, at 0.00008989 g/cm^3. The density of air is 0.00128 g/cm^3.

- **The densest** solid is osmium at 22.59 g/cm^3. Lead is 11.37 g/cm^3. A neutron star has an incredible density of about one billion trillion g/cm^3.

The Curies

- **Pierre and Marie Curie** were the husband and wife scientists who discovered the nature of radioactivity. In 1903 they won a Nobel Prize for their work .

- **Marie Curie** (1867–1934) was born Marya Sklodowska in Poland. She went to Paris in 1891 to study physics.

- **Pierre Curie** (1859–1906) was a French lecturer in physics who discovered the piezoelectric effect in crystals. His discovery led to the development of devices from quartz watches to microphones.

- **The Curies** met in 1894 while Marie was a student at the Sorbonne. They married in 1895.

- **In 1896** Antoine Becquerel found that uranium salts emitted a mysterious radiation that affected photographic paper in the same way as light.

- **In 1898** the Curies found the intensity of radiation was in exact proportion to the amount of uranium—so it must be coming from the uranium atoms.

- **The Curies called** atomic radiation "radioactivity."

- **In July 1898** the Curies discovered a new radioactive element. Marie called it polonium after her native Poland.

- **In December** the Curies found radium—an element even more radioactive than uranium.

- **In 1906** Pierre was killed by a tram. Marie died later from the effects of her exposure to radioactive materials, the dangers of which were unknown at that time.

▶ The Curies' combination of brilliant insight with exact, patient work led to their historic breakthrough in discovering radioactivity.

Hydrogen

▲ Hydrogen's combination with oxygen in water makes it one of the most important elements on the Earth.

- **Hydrogen** is the lightest of all gases. A large swimming pool full of hydrogen would weigh just 2.5lb (1kg).

- **Hydrogen** is the smallest and simplest of all atoms, with just one proton and one electron.

- **Hydrogen** is the first element in the Periodic Table. It has an Atomic Number of 1 and an atomic mass of 1.00794.

- **One in every 6,000** hydrogen atoms has a neutron as well as a proton in its nucleus, making it twice as heavy. This heavy hydrogen atom is called deuterium.

- **Very rare** hydrogen atoms have two neutrons, making them three times as heavy. These are called tritium.

- **Hydrogen** is the most common substance in the Universe, making up over 90 percent of the Universe's weight.

- **Hydrogen** was the first element to form, soon after the Universe began. It was billions of years before any other element formed.

- **Most hydrogen** on Earth occurs in combination with other elements, such as oxygen in water. Pure hydrogen occurs naturally in only a few places, such as small underground pockets and as tiny traces in the air.

- **Hydrogen** is one of the most reactive gases. It bursts easily and often explosively into flames.

- **Under extreme pressure** hydrogen is a metal—the most electrically conductive metal of all.

Quarks

- **Quarks** are one of the three tiniest basic, or elementary, particles from which every substance is made.

- **Quarks** are too small for their size to be measured, but their mass can. The biggest quark, called a top quark, is as heavy as an atom of gold. The smallest, called an up quark, is 35,000 times lighter.

- **There are six** kinds, or flavors, of quark: up (u), down (d), bottom (b), top (t), strange (s), and charm (c).

- **Down, bottom and strange** quarks carry one third of the negative charge of electrons; up, top, and charm ones carry two-thirds of the positive charge of protons.

- **Quarks never exist** separately but in combination with one or two other quarks. Combinations of two or

6 kinds of lepton   6 kinds of quark   6 antiquarks

▶ *These are the main kinds of elementary particle. Besides quarks there are leptons, such as electrons, and antiquarks (the mirror images of quarks).*

Hadrons

Baryons   Mesons

three quarks are called hadrons.

- **Three-quark hadrons** are called baryons and include protons and neutrons. Rare two-quark hadrons are mesons.

- **A proton** is made from two up quarks (two groups of +2/3 of a charge) and one down quark (−1/3) and has a positive charge of 1.

- **A neutron** is made from two down quarks (two groups of −1/3 of a charge) and an up quark (+2/3). The charges cancel each other out, giving a neutron no charge.

- **The theory of quarks** was first proposed by Murray Gell-Mann and Georg Zweig in 1964.

- **Quarks** are named after a famous passage in James Joyce's book *Ulysses*: "Three quarks for Muster Mark!"

Air

- **The air** is a mixture of gases, dust, and moisture.

- **The gas nitrogen** makes up 78.08 percent of the air. Nitrogen is largely unreactive, but it sometimes reacts with oxygen to form oxides of nitrogen.

- **Nitrogen** is continually recycled by the bacteria that consume plant and animal waste.

- **Oxygen** makes up 20.94 percent of the air. Animals

★ STAR FACT ★
Air is a unique mixture that exists on Earth and nowhere else in the solar system.

breathe in oxygen. Plants give it out as they take their energy from sunlight in photosynthesis.

- **Carbon dioxide** makes up 0.03 percent of the air. Carbon dioxide is continually recycled as it is breathed out by animals and taken in by plants in photosynthesis.

- **The air contains** other, inert (unreactive) gases: 0.093 percent is argon; 0.0018 percent is neon; 0.005 percent is helium.

- **There are traces** of krypton and xenon—also inert.

- **Ozone makes up** 0.00006 percent of the air. It is created when sunlight breaks up oxygen.

- **Hydrogen makes up** 0.00005 percent of the air. This gas is continually drifting off into space.

Relativity

- **Einstein** (see Einstein) was the creator of two theories of relativity which have revolutionized scientists' way of thinking about the Universe: the special theory of relativity (1905) and the general theory (1915).

- **Time is relative** because it depends where you measure it from (see Time). Distances and speed are relative too. If you are in a car and another car whizes past you, for instance, the slower you are traveling, the faster the other car seems to be moving.

- **Einstein showed** in his special theory of relativity that you cannot even measure your speed relative to a beam of light, which is the fastest thing in the Universe. This is because light always passes you at the same speed, no matter where you are or how fast you are going.

> ★ STAR FACT ★
> When astronauts went to the Moon, their clock lost a few seconds. The clock was not faulty, but time actually ran slower in the speeding spacecraft.

- **Einstein** realized that if light always travels at the same speed, there are some strange effects when you are moving very fast (see below).

- **If a rocket** passing you zoomed up to near the speed of light, you would see it shrink lengthways.

- **If a rocket** passing you zoomed up to near the speed of light, you'd see the clocks on the rocket running more slowly as time stretched out. If the rocket reached the speed of light, the clocks would stop altogether.

- **If a rocket** accelerates towards the speed of light, its mass increases dramatically. But it gradually becomes so heavy, there isn't enough energy in the Universe to speed it up any further.

- **Einstein's general relativity theory** brought in gravity. It showed that gravity works basically by bending space–time. From this theory scientists predicted black holes (see Hawking) and wormholes (see Time travel).

- **In 1919** an eclipse of the Sun allowed Arthur Eddington to observe how the Sun bends light rays, proving Einstein's theory of General Relativity.

▼ In normal everyday life, the effects of relativity are so tiny that you can ignore them. However, in a spacecraft traveling very fast they may become quite significant.

▲ In a spacecraft traveling almost at the speed of light, time runs slower. So astronauts going on a long, very fast journey into space would come back a little younger than if they had stayed on the Earth.

◀ A spacecraft traveling almost at the speed of light seems to shrink. Of course, if you were actually on board everything would seem entirely normal. Instead, it would be the world outside that seemed to shrink, since it is traveling almost at the speed of light relative to you.

◀ In a spacecraft traveling almost at the speed of light, everything becomes a little heavier. Many scientists believe an object will never be able to accelerate to the speed of light because the faster it goes the heavier it gets. Even in a fast-moving lift, things become very marginally heavier.

Hawking

◀ Stephen Hawking is one of the most famous living scientists. His computer-simulated voice is familiar on many TV science programs.

- **Stephen Hawking** (b.1942) is a British physicist who is famous for his ideas on space and time.

- **Hawking was born** in Oxford, England and studied at Cambridge University, where he is now a professor.

- **Hawking suffers** from the paralyzing nerve disease called amyotrophic lateral sclerosis. He cannot move any more than a few hand and face muscles, but he gets around very well in an electric wheelchair.

- **Hawking cannot speak,** but he communicates effectively with a computer-simulated voice.

- **Hawking's** book A Brief History of Time (1988) outlines his ideas on space, time and the history of the Universe since the Big Bang. It was one of the bestselling science books of the 20th century.

- **Hawking's contributions** to the study of gravity are considered to be the most important since Einstein's.

- **More than anyone else,** Hawking has developed the idea of black holes—points in space where gravity becomes so extreme that it even sucks in light.

- **Hawking developed** the idea of a singularity, which is an incredibly small point in a black hole where all physical laws break down.

- **Hawking's work** provides a strong theoretical base for the idea that the Universe began with a Big Bang, starting with a singularity and exploding outward.

- **Hawking** is trying to find a quantum theory of gravity (see Quantum physics) to link in with the three other basic forces (electromagnetism and nuclear forces).

Oil

- **Oils** are liquids that do not dissolve in water and burn easily.

- **Oils are usually made** from long chains of carbon and hydrogen atoms.

- **There are three main kinds of oil:** essential, fixed, and mineral oils.

- **Essential oils** are thin, perfumed oils from plants. They are used in flavoring and aromatherapy.

▲ Oil from underground and undersea sediments provides over half the world's energy needs.

> ★ STAR FACT ★
> Petroleum is used to make products from aspirins and toothpaste to CDs, as well as gasoline.

- **Fixed oils** are made by plants and animals from fatty acids. They include fish oils and nut and seed oils.

- **Mineral oils** come from petroleum formed underground over millions of years from the remains of shellfish.

- **Petroleum,** or crude oil, is made mainly of hydrocarbons. These are compounds made only of hydrogen and carbon, such as methane (see Carbon).

- **Hydrocarbons** in petroleum are mixed with oxygen, sulphur, nitrogen, and other elements.

- **Petroleum** is separated by distillation into various substances such as aviation fuel, gasoline, and paraffin. As oil is heated in a distillation column, a mixture of gases evaporates. Each gas cools and condenses at different heights to a liquid, or fraction, which is then drawn off.

Scanners

- **Scanners** are electronic devices that move backward and forward in lines in order to build up a picture.

- **Image scanners** are used to convert pictures and other material into a digital form for computers to read.

- **A photoelectric cell** in the scanner measures the amount of light reflected from each part of the picture and converts it into a digital code.

- **Various complex scanners** are used in medicine to build up pictures of the inside of the body. They include CT scanners, PET scanners, and MRI scanners.

- **CT stands** for computerized tomography. An X-ray beam rotates around the patient and is picked up by detectors on the far side to build up a 3-D picture.

- **PET** stands for Positron Emission Tomography. The scanner picks up positrons (positively charged electrons) sent out by radioactive substances injected into the blood.

- **PET scans** can show a living brain in action.

- **MRI** stands for Magnetic Resonance Imaging.

▲ This PET scan shows a monkey's brain from above.

- **An MRI scan** works like CT scans but it uses magnetism, not X-rays. The patient is surrounded by such powerful magnets that all the body's protons (see Atoms) line up.

- **The MRI scan begins** as a radio pulse that knocks the protons briefly out of alignment. The scanner detects radio signals sent out by the protons as they snap back into line.

Vectors

- **For scientists,** vectors are things that have both a particular size and a particular direction.

- **Forces** such as gravity, muscles, or the wind are vector quantities.

- **Acceleration** is a vector quantity.

- **Scalar quantities** are things which have a particular size but have no particular direction.

- **Speed, density, and mass** are all scalar quantities.

- **Velocity** is speed in a particular direction, so it is a vector quantity.

- **A vector** can be drawn on a diagram with an arrow that is proportional in length to its size, pointing in the right direction.

- **Several vectors** may affect something at the same time. As you sit on a chair, gravity pulls you downward, while the chair pushes you up, so you stay still. But if someone pushes the chair from behind, you may tip over. The combined effect of all the forces involved is called the resultant.

- **When several vectors** affect the same thing, they may act at different angles. You can figure out their combined effect—the resultant—by drawing geometric diagrams with the vectors.

- **The parallelogram of forces** is a simple geometric diagram for working out the resultant from two forces. A vector arrow is drawn for each force from the same point. A parallel arrow is then drawn from the end of each arrow to make a parallelogram. The resultant is the simple diagonal of the parallelogram.

◀ As a gymnast pauses in mid-routine, she unconsciously combines the forces acting on her to keep her in balance. These forces, such as her weight and forward momentum, are all vectors and could be figured out geometrically on paper.

Genetic engineering

Donor DNA

DNA plasmid
greatly magnified

1. Cutting out the gene

Gene

2. Breaking open the plasmid

Opened plasmid

3. Splicing the gene
into the plasmid

Bacteria

Bacteria's
ordinary DNA

Altered DNA plasmid
less magnified

4. Bacteria with altered
DNA multiplying

! NEWS FLASH !
In late 1999, scientists figured out the first complete gene sequence for an organism— allowing them to create a new organism entirely artificially.

◀ This illustration shows the steps in gene splicing: 1. The bit of the donor DNA carrying the right gene is snipped out using restriction enzymes. 2. A special ring of DNA called a plasmid is then broken open. 3. The new gene is spliced into the plasmid, which is sealed up with DNA ligase and introduced into bacteria. 4. The bacteria then reproduce.

- **Genetic engineering** means deliberately altering the genes of plants and animals to give them slightly different life instructions.

- **Genes** are found in every living cell on special molecules called DNA (deoxyribonucleic acid). Engineering genes means changing the DNA.

- **Scientists alter genes** by snipping them from the DNA of one organism and inserting them into the DNA of another. This is called gene splicing. The altered DNA is called recombinant DNA.

- **Genes are cut** from DNA using biological scissors called restriction enzymes. They are spliced into DNA using biological glue called DNA ligase.

- **Once a cell** has its new DNA, every time the cell reproduces the new cells will have the same altered DNA.

◀ In 1997, Ian Wilmut and his colleagues in Edinburgh, Scotland, created Dolly the sheep, the first clone of an adult mammal. Many scientists believe it will not be long before the first human clone is made.

- **By splicing new genes** into the DNA of bacteria, scientists can turn them into factories for making valuable natural chemicals. One protein made like this is interferon, a natural body chemical which protects humans against certain viruses. Enzymes for detergents and melanin for suntan lotion can be made like this too.

- **Scientists are now** finding ways of genetically modifying food crops. Crops may be engineered, for instance, to make them resistant to pests or frost. The first GM food was the "Flavr Savr" tomato, which was introduced by the US biotechnology company Calgene in 1994.

- **Gene therapy** means altering the genes to cure diseases that are inherited from parents or caused by faulty genes.

- **Cloning** means creating an organism with exactly the same genes as another. Normally, new life grows from sex cells—cells from both parents—in which genes are mixed. But the DNA in each cell is also a complete set of genes. Cloning takes DNA from any body cell and uses it to grow a new life. Since the new life has the same genes as the donor of the DNA, it is a perfect living replica.

Mixing colors

- **White light** such as sunlight contains all the colors of the rainbow: red, orange, yellow, green, blue, indigo, and violet—and colors between.

- **There are three basic,** or primary colors of light—red, green, and blue. They can be mixed in various proportions to make any other color.

- **The primary colors** of light are called additive primaries, because they are added together to make different colors.

- **Each additive primary** is one third of the full spectrum of white light, so adding all three together makes white.

- **When two additive primaries** are added together they make a third color, called a subtractive primary.

- **The three subtractive primaries are:** magenta (red plus blue), cyan (blue plus green), and yellow (green plus red).

◀ *These circles are the primary colors of light: red, green, and blue. Where they overlap, you see the three subtractive primaries: magenta, cyan, and yellow.*

They too can be mixed to make all the other colors.

- **Colored surfaces** such as painted walls and pictures get their color from the light falling on them. They soak up some colors of white light and reflect the rest. The color you see is the color reflected.

- **With reflected colors,** each subtractive primary soaks up one third of the spectrum of white light and reflects two-thirds of it. Mixing two subtractive primaries soaks up two-thirds of the spectrum. Mixing all three subtractive primaries soaks up all the spectrum, making black.

- **Two subtractive primaries** mixed make an additive primary.

- **Cyan and magenta** make blue; yellow and cyan make green; yellow and magenta make red.

Velocity and acceleration

- **Velocity** is speed in a particular direction.

- **Uniform velocity** is when the velocity stays the same. It can be figured out simply by dividing the distance traveled (d) by the time (t): $v = d/t$.

- **Acceleration** is a change in velocity.

- **Positive acceleration** is getting faster; negative acceleration, or deceleration, is getting slower.

- **Acceleration** is typically given in meters per second per second, or m/sec². This means that in each second it gets faster by one meter per second.

- **A rifle bullet** accelerates down the barrel at 3,000m/sec². A fast car accelerates at 6m/sec².

- **When an object falls,** the Earth's gravity makes it accelerate at 9.81m/sec². This is called g.

- **Acceleration** is often described in gs.

- **In a rocket taking off** at 1g, the acceleration has little effect. But at 3g, it is impossible to move your arms and legs; at 4.5g you black out in five seconds.

- **A high-speed elevator** goes up at 0.2g. An airplane takes off at 0.5g. A car brakes at up to 0.7g. In a crash, you may be able to survive a momentary deceleration of up to 100g, but the effects are likely to be severe.

▶ *For a brief moment sprinters accelerate faster than a Ferrari car.*

Organic chemistry

- **Organic chemistry** is the study of compounds that contain carbon atoms.

- **Over 90 percent** of all chemical compounds are organic.

- **Organic chemicals** are the basis of most life processes.

- **Scientists once thought** carbon compounds could only be made by living things. However, in 1828, Friedrich Wöhler made the compound urea in his laboratory.

- **By far the largest** group of carbon compounds are the hydrocarbons (see Oil).

- **Aliphatic organic compounds** are formed from long or branching chains of carbon atoms. They include ethane, propane, and paraffin, and the alkenes from which many polymers are made (see Oil compounds).

- **Cyclic organic compounds** are formed from closed rings of carbon atoms.

- **Aromatics** are made from a ring of six atoms (mostly carbon), with hydrogen atoms attached. They get their name from the strong aroma (smell) of benzene.

- **Benzene** is the most important aromatic. Friedrich von Stradowitz discovered benzene's ring structure in 1865, after dreaming about a snake biting its own tail.

- **Isomers** are compounds with the same atoms but different properties. Butane and 2-methyl propane in bottled gas are isomers.

▼ All living things are made basically of carbon compounds.

Color

- **Color is the way** our eyes see different wavelengths of light (see Electromagnetic spectrum).

- **Red light** has the longest waves—about 700 nanometres, or nm (billionths of a foot).

- **Violet light** has the shortest waves—about 400nm.

- **Light that is a mixture** of every color, such as sunlight and the light from flashlights and ordinary lightbulbs, is called white light (see Mixing colors).

◄ The macaw gets its brilliant colors because pigment molecules in its feathers soak up certain wavelengths of light and reflect others, including reds, yellows, and blues, very strongly.

- **Things are different colors** because molecules in their surface reflect and absorb certain wavelengths of light.

- **Deep-blue printers inks** and bright-red blood are vividly colored because both have molecules shaped like four-petaled flowers, with a metal atom at the center.

- **Iridescence** is the shimmering rainbow colors you see flashing every now and then on a peacock's feathers, a fly's wings, oil on the water's surface, or a CD.

- **Iridescence** can be caused by the way a surface breaks the light into colors like a prism does (see Spectrum).

- **Iridescence** can be also caused by interference when an object has a thin, transparent surface layer. Light waves reflected from the top surface are slightly out of step with waves reflected from the inner surface, and they interfere.

> ★ STAR FACT ★
> As a light source gets hotter, so its color changes from red to yellow to white to blue.

Motion

- **Every movement** in the Universe is governed by the laws of motion devised by Isaac Newton.

- **Newton's first law of motion** says that an object accelerates or slows down only when a force is applied.

- **Newton's second law of motion** says that the acceleration depends on how heavy the object is, and on how hard it is being pushed or pulled.

- **The greater the force** acting on an object, the more it will accelerate.

- **The heavier an object is**—the greater its mass—the less it will be accelerated by a particular force.

- **Newton's third law of motion** says that when a force pushes or acts one way, an equal force pushes in the opposite direction.

◀ To start moving, a skater uses the force of his muscles to push against the ground. As he or she pushes, the ground pushes back with equal force.

- **Newton's third law of motion** is summarized as follows: "To every action, there is an equal and opposite reaction."

- **Newton's third law** applies everywhere, but you can see it in effect in a rocket in space. In space there is nothing for the rocket to push on. The rocket is propelled by the action and reaction between the hot gases pushed out by its engines and the rocket itself.

- **You cannot always see** the reaction. When you bounce a ball on the ground, it looks as if only the ball bounces, but the Earth recoils too. The Earth's mass is so great compared to the ball's that the recoil is tiny.

- **Einstein's theory** of relativity modifies Newton's second law of motion under certain circumstances.

Molecules

- **A molecule** is two or more atoms bonded together. It is normally the smallest bit of a substance that exists separately.

- **Hydrogen atoms** exist only in pairs, or joined with atoms of other elements. A linked pair of hydrogen atoms is a hydrogen molecule.

- **The atoms in a molecule** are held together by chemical bonds (see Chemical bonds).

★ STAR FACT ★
If the DNA molecules in human body cells was as thick as a hair, it would be 5mi (8km) long.

- **The shape of a molecule** depends on the arrangement of bonds that hold its atoms together.

- **Ammonia molecules** are pyramid shaped; protein molecules are long spirals.

- **Compounds** only exist as molecules. If the atoms in the molecule of a compound were separated, the compound would cease to exist.

- **Chemical formulas** show the atoms in a molecule.

- **The formula for ammonia**, a choking gas, is NH_3, because it is made from three hydrogen atoms and one nitrogen atom.

- **The mass of a molecule** is called the molecular mass. It is determined by adding the mass of all the atoms in it.

◀ A crystal such as this is built from billions of identical molecules.

Space

- **A flat, or plane, surface** has just two dimensions at right angles to each other: length and width.

- **Any point** on a flat surface can be pinpointed exactly with just two figures: one showing how far along it is and the other how far across.

- **There are three** dimensions of space at right angles to each other: length, width, and height.

- **A box** can be described completely with just one figure for each dimension.

- **A point in space** can be pinpointed with three figures: one shows how far along it is, one how far

▶ *An eclipse of the Sun in 1919 showed Einstein's suggestion that gravity can bend light is true. In bending light, gravity is also bending space–time.*

across it is and a third how high up or down it is.

- **If something is moving**, three dimensions are not enough to locate it. You need a fourth dimension—time—to describe where the object is at a particular time.

- **In the early 1900s,** mathematician Hermann Minkowski realized that for Einstein's relativity theory you had to think of the Universe in terms of four dimensions, including time.

  - **Four-dimensional** space is now called space–time.

  - **Einstein's** theory of general relativity shows that space–time is actually curved.

  - **After Minkowski's ideas,** mathematicians began to develop special geometry to describe four or even more dimensions.

Elements

- **Elements** are the basic chemicals of the Universe. Each element is made from only one kind of atom, with a certain number of protons and its own unique character.

- **More than 115** elements have so far been identified.

- **Each element** is listed in the periodic table.

- **At least 20** of the most recently identified elements were created entirely by scientists and do not exist naturally.

> **! NEWS FLASH !**
> Scientists in Berkeley, California, have made three atoms of a new element, ununoctium, which is probably a colorless gas.

- **All the most recently discovered elements** have very large, heavy atoms.

- **The lightest atom** is hydrogen.

- **The densest naturally occurring element** is osmium.

- **When different elements combine** they make chemical compounds (see Chemical compounds).

- **New elements** get their name from their atomic number (see The Periodic Table). So the new element with atomic number 116 is called ununhexium. Un is the Latin word for one; *hex* is Latin for six.

◀ *Very few elements occur naturally by themselves. Most occur in combination with others in compounds. Gold is one of the few elements found as a pure "native" element.*

Light

▶ This straw is not a light source, so we see it by reflected light. As the light rays reflected from the straw leave the water, they are bent, or refracted, as they emerge from the water and speed up. So the straw looks broken even though it remains intact.

● **Light is a form of energy.** It is one of the forms of energy sent out by atoms when they become excited.

● **Light is just one** of the forms of electromagnetic radiation (see Electromagnetic spectrum). It is the only form that we can see.

● **Although we are surrounded** by light during the day, very few things give out light. The Sun and other stars and electric lights are light sources, but we see most things only because they reflect light. If something does not send out or reflect light, we cannot see it.

● **Light beams** are made of billions of tiny packets of energy called photons (see Moving light). Together, these photons behave like waves on a pond. But the waves are tiny—2,000 would fit across a pinhead.

● **Light travels** in straight lines. The direction can be changed when light bounces off something or passes through it, but it is always straight. The straight path of light is called a ray.

● **When the path of a light ray** is blocked altogether, it forms a shadow. Most shadows have two regions: the umbra and penumbra. The umbra is the dark part where light rays are blocked altogether. The penumbra is the lighter rim where some rays reach.

● **When light rays** hit something, they bounce off, are soaked up, or pass through. Anything that lets light through, such as glass, is transparent. If it mixes the light on the way through, such as frosted glass, it is translucent. If it stops light altogether, it is opaque.

● **When light strikes a surface**, some or all of it is reflected. Most surfaces scatter light in all directions, and all you see is the surface. But mirrors and other shiny surfaces reflect light in exactly the same pattern in which it arrived, so you see a mirror image.

● **When light passes** into transparent things such as water, rays are bent, or refracted. This happens because light travels more slowly in glass or water, and the rays swing around like the wheels of a car running onto sand.

▶ Glass lenses are shaped to refract light rays in particular ways. Concave lenses are dish-shaped lenses—thin in the middle and fat at the edges. As light rays pass through a concave lens they are bent outward, so they spread out. The result is that when you see an object through a concave lens, it looks smaller than it really is.

▶ Convex lenses bulge outward. They are fatter in the middle and thin around the edges. As light rays pass through a convex lens they are bent inward, so they come together, or converge. When you see an object through a convex lens, it looks magnified. The point where the converging light rays meet is called the focus.

What you see is not the object itself but a reduced image

How the light rays look to you

Light rays spread out

The object

Light rays from the object

Concave lens cut in half

What you see is not the object itself but a magnified image

How the light rays look to you

Light rays converge

The object

Light rays from the object

Convex lens cut in half

Television

▲ *TV cameras convert a scene into an electrical signal.*

- **Television relies** on the photoelectric effect—emissions of electrons by a substance when struck by photons of light. Light-sensitive photocells in cameras work like this.

- **TV cameras** have three sets of tubes with photocells (reacting to red, green, and blue light) to convert the picture into an electrical signal.

- **The sound signal** from microphones is added, and a "sync pulse" is put in to keep both signals in time.

- **The combined signal** is turned into radio waves (see Electromagnetic spectrum) and broadcast.

- **An antenna** picks up the signal and feeds it to your television set.

- **Most TV sets** are based on glass tubes shaped like giant lightbulbs, called cathode-ray tubes. The narrow end contains a cathode, which is a negative electrical terminal. The wide end is the TV screen.

- **The cathode** fires a non-stop stream of electrons (see Electrons) at the inside of the TV screen.

- **Wherever electrons** hit the screen, the screen glows as its coating of phosphors heats up.

- **To build up the picture** the electron beam scans quickly back and forth across the screen, making it glow in certain places. This happens so quickly that it looks as if the whole screen is glowing.

- **Color TVs** have three electron guns: one to make red phosphors glow, another for green, and a third for blue.

Huygens

- **Christiaan Huygens** (1629–1695) was, after Isaac Newton, the greatest scientist of the 1600s.

- **Huygens** was born to a wealthy Dutch family in The Hague, in Holland.

- **He studied law** at the University of Leiden and the College of Orange in Breda before turning to science.

- **He worked** with his brother Constanijn to grind lenses for very powerful telescopes.

- **With his powerful telescope,** Huygens discovered in 1655 that what astronomers had thought were Saturn's "arms" were actually rings. He made his discovery known to people in code.

- **Huygens discovered** Titan, one of Saturn's moons.

◀ *Christiaan Huygens was the leading figure of the Golden Age of Dutch science in the 17th century, making contributions in many fields.*

- **Huygens learned a great deal** about pendulums and built the first accurate pendulum clock.

- **Responding to Newton's theory** that light was "corpuscles," Huygens developed the theory that light is waves (see Moving light) in 1678.

- **Huygens** described light as vibrations spreading through a material called ether, which is literally everywhere and is made of tiny particles. The idea of ether was finally abandoned in the late 19th century, but not the idea of light waves.

- **Huygens' wave idea** enabled him to explain refraction (see Light) simply. It also enabled him to predict that light would travel more slowly in glass than in air.

Engines

- **Engines are devices** that convert fuel into movement.

- **Most engines** work by burning the fuel to make gases that expand rapidly as they get hot.

- **Engines** that burn fuel to generate power are called heat engines. The burning is called combustion.

- **An internal combustion** engine, as used in a car, a jet, or a rocket, burns its fuel on the inside.

▶ The Thrust car used a rocket motor to give it the acceleration it needed for its attempt on the world land speed record.

- **In engines** such as those in cars and diesel trains, the hot gases swell inside a chamber (the combustion chamber) and push against a piston or turbine.

- **An external combustion** engine burns its fuel on the outside in a separate boiler that makes hot steam to drive a piston or turbine. Steam engines on trains and boats work in this way.

- **Engines with pistons** that go back and forth inside cylinders are called reciprocating engines.

- **In jets and rockets,** hot gases swell and push against the engine as they shoot out of the back.

- **In four-stroke engines,** such as those in most cars, the pistons go up and down four times for each time they are thrust down by the hot gases.

- **In two-stroke engines,** such as those on small motorcycles, lawnmowers, and chainsaws, the piston is pushed by burning gases every time it goes down.

Solutions and mixtures

- **Tap water** is rarely pure water; it usually contains invisible traces of other substances. This makes it a solution.

- **A solution** is a liquid that has a solid dissolved within it.

- **When a solid dissolves,** its molecules separate and mix completely with the molecules of the liquid.

- **The liquid** in a solution is called the solvent.

- **The solid** dissolved in a solution is the solute.

- **The more of a solid that dissolves**, the stronger the solution becomes until at last it is saturated and no more will dissolve. There is literally no more room in the liquid.

- **If a saturated** solution is heated the liquid expands, making room for more solute to dissolve.

> ★ STAR FACT ★
> Ancient alchemists searched for a universal solvent in which all substances would dissolve.

▶ Seawater is a solution containing a huge range of dissolved substances. They include simple salt (sodium chloride) and magnesium chloride, but most are in very tiny amounts.

- **If a saturated** solution cools or is left to evaporate there is less room for solute, so the solute is precipitated (comes out of the solution).

- **Precipitated solute** molecules often link together to form solid crystals.

Nuclear power

- **Nuclear power** is based on the huge amounts of energy that bind together the nucleus of every atom in the Universe. It is an incredibly concentrated form of energy.

- **Nuclear energy** is released by splitting the nuclei of atoms in a process called nuclear fission (see Nuclear energy). One day scientists hope to release energy by nuclear fusion, by fusing nuclei together as in the Sun.

- **Most nuclear reactors** use uranium-235. These are special atoms, or isotopes, of uranium with 235 protons and neutrons in their nucleus rather than the normal 238.

- **The fuel** usually consists of tiny pellets of uranium dioxide in thin tubes, separated by sheets called spacers.

- **Six and a half pounds of uranium fuel** provide enough energy for a city of one million people for one day.

▼ *Like coal- and oil-fired power stations, nuclear power stations use steam to drive turbines to generate electricity. The difference is that nuclear power stations obtain the heat by splitting uranium atoms, not by burning coal or oil. When the atom is split, it sends out gamma rays, neutrons, and immense heat. In a nuclear bomb this happens in a split second. In a nuclear power plant, control rods soak up some of the neutrons and slow the process down.*

- **The earliest reactors,** called N-reactors, were designed to make plutonium for bombs. Magnox reactors make both plutonium and electricity.

- **Pressurized water reactors** (PWRs), originally used in submarines, are now the most common kind. They are built in factories, unlike Advanced Gas Reactors (AGRs).

- **Fast-breeder reactors** actually create more fuel than they burn, but the new fuel is highly radioactive.

- **Every stage of the nuclear process** creates dangerous radioactive waste. The radioactivity may take 80,000 years to fade. All but the most radioactive liquid waste is pumped out to sea. Gaseous waste is vented into the air. Solid waste is mostly stockpiled underground. Scientists debate fiercely about what to do with radioactive waste.

> ★ STAR FACT ★
> One kilogram of deuterium (a kind of hydrogen) can give the same amount of energy as three million kilograms of coal.

Control rods slow the process down by absorbing neutrons

A "moderator" such as graphite slows down the neutrons so that they hit more nuclei, making the most of the fuel

The electricity is distributed across the country through high-voltage power lines

Raging hot air from the reactor turns water in the pipe into steam

A transformer boosts the voltage ready for transmission

As the turbines spin, they drive magnets around inside electric coils to generate electricity

The steam is blasted over turbines, driving them around

Uranium fuel rods give off heat

Concrete surrounds the reactor

The steam is cooled to water and cycled back to the reactor

Moving particles

- **The tiny molecules** from which every substance is made are always moving.

- **The speed** at which molecules move depends on temperature.

- **Heat gives molecules** extra energy, making them move faster.

- **In 1827** Scottish botanist Robert Brown saw through a microscope that pollen grains in water were constantly dancing. They are buffeted by moving molecules that are too small to be seen. The effect is called Brownian motion.

- **In a gas,** the molecules are so far apart that they zoom around freely in all directions.

- **Smells spread** quickly because the smell molecules move around quickly.

◀ As liquids boil, the molecules move around more and more energetically until some break away altogether and turn to gas. This is called evaporation.

- **In a liquid,** molecules are closely packed and move like dancers in a nightclub. If molecules stopped moving in liquids we would all die, because this molecular movement is what moves materials in and out of human cells.

- **In a solid**, molecules and atoms are bound together and vibrate on the spot.

- **Air and water pressure** is simply bombardment by billions of moving molecules.

- **At 459.67°F (–273°C),** which is called absolute zero, the movement of atoms and molecules slows down to a complete standstill.

Inertia and momentum

- **Everything that is standing still** has inertia, which means that it will not move unless forced to.

- **Everything that moves** has momentum, which means that it will not slow down or speed up unless forced to.

- **There is no real difference** between inertia and momentum, because everything in the universe is moving. Things only appear to be still because they are not moving relative to something else.

- **An object's momentum** is its mass times its velocity.

- **Something heavy** or fast has a lot of momentum, so a large force is needed to slow it down or speed it up.

- **A ball moves** when you kick it because when a moving object strikes another, its momentum is transferred. This is the law of conservation of momentum.

- **Angular momentum** is the momentum of something spinning. It depends on its speed and the size of the circle.

- **When a spinning skater** draws his arms close to his body, the circle he is making is smaller yet his angular momentum must be the same. So he spins faster.

- **A satellite** orbiting close to the Earth travels faster than one orbiting farther out.

- **A spinning top stays** upright because its angular momentum is greater than the pull of gravity.

▼ The lead shot that athletes throw when they put the shot has a large mass. It takes a lot of muscle power to overcome its inertia.

The Internet

- **The Internet** is a vast network linking millions of computers around the world.

- **The Internet began** in the 1960s when the U.S. Army developed a network called ARPAnet to link computers.

- **To access the Internet** a computer's output is translated into a form that can be sent by phone lines with a modem (short for modulator/demodulator).

- **Computers** access the Internet via a local phone to a large computer called the Internet Service Provider (ISP).

- **Each ISP** is connected to a giant computer called a main hub. There are about 100 linked main hubs worldwide.

- **Some links between** hubs are made via phone lines; some are made via satellite.

- **Links between** hubs are called fast-track connections.

> **! NEWS FLASH !**
> It is now possible to access the Internet
> via mobile phones.

▶ *The Internet links computers instantly around the world.*

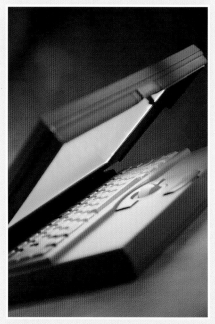

- **The World Wide Web** is a way of finding your way to the data in sites on all the computers linked to the Internet. The Web makes hyperlinks (fast links) to sites with the word you select.

- **The World Wide Web** was invented in 1989 by Tim Berners-Lee of the CERN laboratories in Switzerland.

Temperature

- **Temperature** is how hot or cold something is. The best-known temperature scales are Celsius and Fahrenheit.

- **The Celsius (C) scale** is part of the metric system of measurements and is used everywhere except in the U.S.A. It is named after Swedish astronomer Anders Celsius, who developed it in 1742.

- **Celsius is also** known as centigrade because water boils at 100°C. *Cent* is the Latin prefix for 100. Water freezes at 0°C.

- **On the Fahrenheit (F) scale** water boils at 212°F. It freezes at 32°F.

- **To convert Celsius** to Fahrenheit, divide by 5, multiply by 9 and add 32.

- **To convert Fahrenheit** to Celsius, subtract 32, divide by 9 and multiply by 5.

◀ *A digital thermometer measures temperature with a thermistor, which is a probe whose electrical resistance varies with the heat.*

- **The Kelvin (K) scale** used by scientists is like the Celsius scale, but it begins at −273.15°C. So 0°C is 273.15K.

- **Cold:** absolute zero is −459.6°F (273.15°C). The coldest teperature ever obtained in a laboratory is −523.398°F (272.99999°C). Helium turns liquid at −452.2°F (−269°C). Oxygen turns liquid at −297.4°F (−183°C). The lowest air temperature ever recorded on Earth is −128.56°F (−89.2°C).

- **Hot:** the highest shade temperature recorded on Earth is 136.4°F (58°C). The surface of the Sun is around 10,830°F (6,000°C). The center of the Earth is over 12,600°F (7,000°C). A lightning flash reaches 54,000°F (30,000°C). The center of a hydrogen bomb reaches 7 million°F.

- **The blood temperature** of the human body is normally 98.6°F (37°C). A skin temperature above 104°F (40°C) is very hot, and below 87.8°F 31°C) is very cold. Hands feel cold below 68°F (20°C) and go numb below 53°F (12°C). Anything above 113°F (45°C) touching your skin hurts, although people have walked on hot coals at 1472°F (800°C).

Newton

- **Sir Isaac Newton** was one of the greatest scientists. His book *The Mathematical Principles of Natural Philosophy* is the most influential science book ever written.

- **Newton was born** on December 25, 1642 in Woolsthorpe in Lincoln, England. As a boy, he often made mechanical devices such as model windmills and water clocks.

- **With his theory of gravity** Newton discovered how the Universe is held together.

- **Newton** said that his theory of gravity was inspired by seeing an apple fall from a tree when he left Cambridge to escape the plague.

- **Newton invented** an entirely new branch of mathematics called calculus. Independently, Leibniz also invented it.

- **Newton** discovered that sunlight is a mixture of all colors (see Spectrum).

- **His greatest achievement** was his laws of motion.

- **Newton** spent much of his life studying astrology and alchemy.

- **Newton never married** and at times was almost a recluse. Shortly before he died in 1727 he said: "I seem to have been only like a boy playing on the seashore, and diverting myself in now and then finding a smoother pebble or prettier shell than ordinary, whilst the great ocean of truth lay all undiscovered before me."

- **Newton** was a Member of Parliament, president of the Royal Society, and master of the Royal Mint, where he found a way to make coins more accurately.

▶ *Newton invented a kind of telescope that is now standard for astronomers.*

Moving light

- **Light is the fastest thing** in the Universe.

- **The speed of light** is 299,792,458 meters per second.

- **Scientists recall** light's metric speed from the number of letters in each word of this sentence: "We guarantee certainty, clearly referring to this light mnemonic."

- **Isaac Newton** suggested in 1666 that light is made up of streams of tiny particles, or corpuscles.

- **The Dutch scientist** Christiaan Huygens (1629–95) said

in 1678: no, light is waves or vibrations instead.

- **In 1804 Thomas Young** showed that light is waves in a famous experiment with two narrow slits in a light beam. Light coming through each slit creates bands of shadow that must be caused by waves interfering with each other.

- **James Clerk Maxwell** suggested in the 1860s that light is electromagnetic waves.

- **Albert Einstein** showed with the photoelectric effect that light must also be particles called photons.

- **Light sometimes** looks like photons, sometimes like waves. Weirdly, in a way scientists can't explain, a single photon can interfere with itself in Young's slit experiment.

◀ *The shimmering colors on a CD are caused by interfering light waves, where different wavelengths cancel out their peaks and troughs.*

Holograms

- **Holograms** are three-dimensional photographic images made with laser lights.

- **The idea of holograms** was suggested by Hungarian-born British physicist Dennis Gabor in 1947. The idea could not be tried until laser light became available.

- **The first holograms** were made by Emmett Leith and Juris Upatnieks in Michigan in 1963 and by Yuri Denisyuk in the Soviet Union.

- **To make a hologram,** the beam from a laser light is split in two. One part of the beam is reflected off the subject onto a photographic plate. The other, called the reference beam, shines directly onto the plate.

- **The interference** between light waves in the reflected beam and light waves in the reference beam creates the hologram in complex microscopic stripes on the plate.

- **Some holograms** only show up when laser light is shined through them.

- **Some holograms** work in ordinary light, such as those

▲ *Holograms seem to hover strangely in space.*

used in credit cards to stop counterfeiting.

- **Holograms** are used to detect defects in engines and airplanes, and forgeries in paintings by comparing two holograms made under slightly different conditions.

- **Huge amounts of digital data** can be stored in holograms in a crystal.

- **In 1993** 10,000 pages of data were stored in a lithium nobate crystal measuring just 0.4in (1cm) across.

Sound measurement

▲ *Heavy traffic is about 90 decibels, but it can rise higher.*

- **The loudness of a sound** is usually measured in units called decibels (dB).

- **One decibel** is one tenth of a bel, the unit of sound named after Scots-born inventor Alexander Graham Bell.

- **Decibels** were originally used to measure sound intensity. Now they are used to compare electronic power output and voltages too.

- **Every 10 points up** on the decibel scale means that a sound has increased by ten times.

- **1dB** is the smallest change the human ear can hear.

- **The quietest sound** that people can hear is 10dB.

- **Quiet sounds:** a rustle of leaves or a quiet whisper is 10 dB. A quiet conversation is 30–40dB. Loud conversation is about 60 dB. A city street is about 70dB.

- **Loud sounds:** thunder is about 100 dB. The loudest scream ever recorded was 128.4dB. A jet taking off is 110–140dB. The loudest sound ever made by human technology (an atom bomb) was 210dB.

- **The amount of energy** in a sound is measured in watts per square meter (W/m²). Zero dB is one thousand billionths of 1W/m².

> ★ STAR FACT ★
> Sounds over 130dB are painful; sounds over 100dB for long periods cause deafness.

Electrical power

- **Most electricity is generated in power stations** by magnets that spin between coils of wire to induce an electric current (see Electric circuits).

- **The magnets** are turned by turbines, which are themselves turned by steam heated by burning coal, oil, or gas, or by nuclear fuel, or turned by wind or water.

- **The stronger the magnet**, the faster it turns and the more coils there are, so the bigger the voltage created.

- **Simple dynamos** generate a direct current (DC) that always flows in the same direction.

- **The generators** in power stations are alternators that give an alternating current (AC) which continually swaps direction. In an alternator, as the magnets spin they pass the wires going up on one side and down on the other.

- **The system of power transmission** that takes electricity into homes was developed by Croatian-born U.S. engineer Nikola Tesla at Niagara in the 1880s.

- **Electricity from power stations** is distributed around a country in a network of cables known as the grid.

- **Power station** generators push out 25,000 volts or more. This voltage is too much to use in people's homes, but not enough to transmit over long distances.

- **To transmit** electricity over long distances, the voltage is boosted to 400,000 volts by step-up transformers. It is fed through high-voltage cables. Near its destination the electricity's voltage is reduced by step-down transformers at substations for distribution to homes, stores, offices, and factories.

▼ Electricity is brought to our homes through a network of high-tension cables. Some cables are buried underground, some are suspended high in the air from metal towers called pylons.

Pylon

High-voltage power lines from power stations

Substation

A step-down transformer reduces the voltage further to 110 volts for homes

A step-down transformer at the substation reduces the voltage to 800 volts

Factories often need a 460-volt electric current

Copper

▲ The high conductivity of copper makes it a perfect material for the core of electrical cables.

- **Copper** was one of the first metals used by humans over 10,000 years ago.

- **Copper** is one of the few metals that occur naturally in a pure form.

- **Most of the copper** that we use today comes from ores such as cuprite and chalcopyrite.

- **The world's biggest deposits** of pure copper are in volcanic lavas in the Andes Mountains in Chile.

- **Copper has** the atomic number 29, an atomic mass of 63.546, and melts at 1,981.4°F (1,083°C).

- **Copper is** by far the best low-cost conductor of electricity, so it is widely used for electrical cables.

- **Copper is also** a good conductor of heat, which is why it is used to make saucepans and heating pipes.

- **Copper is so ductile** (easily stretched) that a copper rod as thick as a finger can be stretched out thinner than a human hair.

- **After being in the air** for some time, copper gets a thin green coating of copper carbonate called verdigris. "Verdigris" means green of Greece.

> ★ **STAR FACT** ★
> Copper is mixed with tin to make bronze, the oldest of all alloys dating back 5,000 years.

Energy

- **Energy is the ability** to make things happen or, as scientists say, do work.

- **Energy comes in many forms,** from the chemical energy locked in sugar to the mechanical energy in a speeding train.

- **Energy does its work** either by transfer or conversion.

▲ Power stations do not create energy. They simply convert it into a convenient form for us to use.

- **Energy transfer** is the movement of energy from one place to another, such as heat rising above a fire or a ball being thrown.

- **Energy conversion** is when energy changes from one form to another—as when wind turbines generate electric power, for instance.

- **Energy is never lost nor gained;** it simply moves or changes. The total amount of energy in the Universe has stayed the same since the dawn of time.

- **Energy and mass** are actually the same thing. They are like flip sides of a coin and are interchangeable.

- **Potential energy** is energy stored up for action—as in a squeezed spring or a stretched piece of elastic.

- **Kinetic energy** is energy that something has because it is moving, such as a rolling ball or a falling stone.

- **Kinetic energy** increases in proportion with the velocity of an object squared. So a car has four times more kinetic energy at 24mph (40km/h) than at 12mph (20km/h).

Thermodynamics

- **Energy cannot be destroyed** but it can be burned up. Every time energy is used, some turns into heat. This is why you feel hot after running.

- **Energy that turns into heat** may not be lost. It dissipates (spreads out thinly in all directions) and is hard to use again.

- **Every time energy is used,** some free energy (energy available to make things happen) gets lost as heat.

- **Scientists use** the word "entropy" to describe how much energy has become unusable. The less free energy there is, the greater the entropy.

- **The word "entropy"** was invented by the German physicist Rudolf Clausius in 1868.

- **Clausius showed** that everything really happens because energy moves from areas of high energy to areas of low energy, from hot areas to cold areas.

◄ ▼ Energy cannot be reused once it has turned to heat and dissipated just as you cannot rebuild an igloo once the snow has melted.

- **Energy goes on flowing** from high to low until there is no difference to make anything happen. This is an equilibrium state. Entropy is the maximum.

- **Clausius summed this idea up** in the 1860s with two laws of thermodynamics.

- **The first law of thermodynamics** says the total energy in the Universe was fixed forever at the beginning of time.

- **The second law of thermodynamics** says that energy is dissipated every time it is used. So the entropy of the Universe must increase.

Sound

- **Most sounds** you hear, from the whisper of the wind to the roar of a jet, are simply moving air. When any sound is made it makes the air vibrate, and these vibrations carry the sound to your ears.

- **The vibrations** that carry sound through the air are called sound waves.

- **Sound waves** move by alternately squeezing air molecules together and then stretching them apart.

- **The parts of the air** that are squeezed are called condensations; the parts of the air that are stretched are called rarefactions.

- **Sound waves** travel faster through liquids and solids than through air because the molecules are more closely packed together in liquids and solids.

- **In a vacuum** such as space there is complete silence because there are no molecules to carry the sound.

- **Sound travels** at about 65ft (344m) per second in air at 68°F (20°C).

- **Sound travels** travels faster in warm air, reaching 1,266ft (386m) per second at 212°F (68°C).

- **Sound travels** at 5,000ft (1,500m) per second in water and at 20,000ft (6,100m) per second in solid teel.

- **Sound travels a million times** slower than light, which is why you hear thunder well after you see a flash of lightning.

► When you sing, talk, or shout, you are actually vibrating the vocal cords in your throat. These set up sound waves in the air you push up from your lungs.

Time travel

- **Einstein showed** that time runs at different speeds in different places—and is just another dimension. Ever since, some scientists have wondered whether we could travel through time to the past or the future (see Time).

- **Einstein said** you cannot move through time because you would have to travel faster than light. If you traveled as fast as light, time would stop and you would not be alive.

- **A famous argument** against time travel is about killing your grandparents. What if you traveled back in time before your parents were born and killed your grandparents? Then neither your parents nor you could have been born. So who killed your grandparents?

- **In the 1930s** American mathematician Kurt Gödel found time travel might be possible by bending space–time.

- **Scientists have come up** with all kinds of weird ideas for bending space–time, including amazing gravity machines. The most powerful benders of space–time are black holes in space.

- **Stephen Hawking** said you cannot use black holes for time travel because everything that goes into a black hole shrinks to a singularity (see Hawking). Others say you might dodge the singularity and emerge somewhere else in the Universe through a reverse black hole called a white hole.

- **U.S. astronomer Carl Sagan** thought small black hole–white hole tunnels might exist without a singularity. There might be tunnels such as these linking different parts of the Universe, like a wormhole in an apple.

- **Mathematicians** say that a wormhole would snap shut as soon as you stepped into it. However, it might be possible to hold it open with an anti-gravity machine based on a quantum effect called the Casimir effect.

- **Stephen Hawking** says wormholes are so unstable that they would break up before you could use them to time travel. Martin Visser says you might use them for faster than light (FTL) travel, but not for time travel.

▼ *If wormholes exist, they are thought to be very, very tiny—smaller than an atom. So how could they be used for time travel? Some scientists think you may be able to use an incredibly powerful electric field to enlarge them and hold them open long enough to make a tunnel through space–time.*

2000

The wormhole time machine depends on blowing a wormhole up large enough and holding it open long enough for you to slip through

Although it's hard to imagine, space–time is not space with stars like this at all. It is a four-dimensional space and traveling through space–time means traveling through time as well as space

The far end of a wormhole is the opposite of a black hole—a white hole. It pushes things out, not sucks them in

1500

If you could create a wormhole time machine, just where and when would the other end be?

! NEWS FLASH !
A new theory called the Many Worlds Theory suggests that at any moment there are many different possible futures—and all of these futures actually happen.

Sound recording

▲ In a recording studio, the sound is recorded either on computer or on big master tapes.

- **Sound is recorded** by using a microphone to turn the vibrations of sound into a varying electrical current.

- **Sound recording** in the past was analog, which means that the electrical current varies continually exactly as the sound vibrations do.

- **Most sound recording** today is digital, which means that sound vibrations are broken into tiny electrical chunks.

- **To make a digital recording** a device called an analog-to-digital converter divides the vibrations into 44,100 segments for each second of sound.

- **Each digital segment** is turned into a digital code of ON or OFF electrical pulses.

- **With analog sound,** each time the signal is passed on to the next stage, distortion and noise are added. With digital sound no noise is added, but the original recording is not a perfect replica of the sound.

- **On a CD (compact disk)** the pattern of electrical pulses is burned by a laser into pits on the surface of the disk.

- **During playback,** a laser beam is reflected from the tiny pits on a CD to re-create the electrical signal.

- **DVDs** work like CDs. They store huge amounts of data on both sides, but most can only be recorded on once.

- **Minidiscs** (MDs) use magneto-optical recording to allow you to record on the disk up to one million times. A laser burns the data into a magnetic pattern on the disk.

Glass

- **Glass** is made mainly from ordinary sand (made of silica), from soda ash (sodium carbonate), and from limestone (calcium carbonate).

- **Glass** can be made from silica alone. However, silica has a very high melting point 3,092°F (1,700°C), so soda ash is added to lower its melting point.

- **Adding a lot of soda ash** makes glass too soluble in water, so limestone is added to reduce its solubility.

- **To glass sheets,** 6 percent lime and 4 percent magnesia (magnesium oxide) are added to the mix.

- **To make glass for bottles,** 2 percent alumina (aluminum oxide) is added to the basic mix.

- **Very cheap glass** is green because it contains small impurities of iron.

> ★ STAR FACT ★
> The person who controls the fires and loads the glass into the furnace is called a teaser.

▲ Glass is one of the most versatile of all materials—transparent, easily molded, and resistant to the weather. This is why it is used in modern buildings such as this addition to the Louvre in Paris.

- **Metallic oxides** are added to make different colors.

- **Unlike most solids,** glass is not made of crystals and does not have the same rigid structure. It is called an amorphous solid.

- **When glass melts** it flows slowly like a thick liquid.

Radiation

- **Radiation** is an atom's way of getting rid of its excess energy.

- **There are two main kinds** of radiation: electromagnetic and particulate.

- **Electromagnetic radiation** is pure energy. It comes from electrons (see Electrons).

- **Particulate radiation** is tiny bits of matter thrown out by the nuclei of atoms.

▲ Exposure to radiation can cause illnesses ranging from nausea to cancer and death. So radioactive materials must be safely guarded.

- **Particulate** radiation comes mainly from radioactive substances (see Radioactivity) such as radium, uranium, and other heavy elements as they break down.

- **Radiation is measured** in curies and becquerels (radiation released), röntgens (victim's exposure), rads and grays (dose absorbed), rems and sieverts (amount of radiation in the body).

- **Bacteria can stand** a radiation dose 10,000 times greater than the dose that would kill a human being.

- **The Chernobyl nuclear accident** released 50 million curies of radiation. A 20-kiloton nuclear bomb releases 10,000 times more radiation.

- **The natural radioactivity** of a brazil nut is about six becquerels (1 ten-millionth of a curie), which means six atoms in the nut break up every second.

- **The natural background** radiation you receive over a year is about 100 times what you receive from a single chest X-ray.

Water

- **Water** is solid, liquid, and gas at normal temperatures. It melts at 32°F (0°C) and boils at 212°F (100°C).

- **Water is at its densest** at 39°F (4°C).

- **Ice is much less dense** than water, which is why ice forms on the surface of ponds and why icebergs float.

- **Water is the only substance** that expands as it freezes, which is why pipes burst during cold winter weather.

- **Water** makes mild solutions with other substances.

- **Water is a compound** made of two hydrogen atoms and one oxygen atom. It has the chemical formula H_2O.

- **A water molecule** is shaped like a flattened V, with the two hydrogen atoms on each tip.

  - **A water molecule** is said to be polar because the oxygen end is more negatively charged electrically.

    - **Similar substances** like ammonia are

◄ A water molecule has two hydrogen atoms and one oxygen atom in a shallow V-shape.

gases to below 32°F (0°C).

- **Water stays liquid** until 212°F (100°C) because pairs of its polar molecules make strong bonds, as the positively charged end of one molecule is drawn to the negatively charged end of another.

▼ Water is found in liquid form in many places, such as rivers, and as a gas in the atmosphere.

Carbon

- **Pure carbon** occurs in four forms: diamond, graphite, amorphous carbon, and fullerenes.

- **Fullerenes** are made mostly artificially, but all four forms of carbon can be made artificially.

- **Diamond** is the world's hardest substance.

- **Natural diamonds** were formed deep in the Earth billions of years ago. They were formed by huge pressures as the Earth's crust moved, and then brought nearer the surface by volcanic activity.

- **Graphite** is the soft black carbon used in pencils. It is soft because it is made from sheets of atoms that slide over each other.

- **Amorphous carbon** is the black soot left behind when candles and other objects burn.

▶ The extraordinary hardness of diamonds comes from the incredibly strong tetrahedron (pyramid shape) that carbon atoms form.

- **Fullerenes** are big molecules made of 60 or more carbon atoms linked together in a tight cylinder or ball. The first was made in 1985.

- **Fullerenes** are named after the architect Buckminster Fuller who designed a geodesic (Earth-shaped) dome.

- **Carbon forms** over one million compounds which form the basis of organic chemistry. It does not react chemically at room temperature. Carbon has the chemical formula C and the atomic number 6. Neither diamond nor graphite melts at normal pressures.

Echoes and acoustics

▶ Sydney Opera House in Australia is famous for its stunning design, but some orchestras have complained about its acoustics.

- **An echo** is the reflection of a sound. You hear it a little while after the sound is made.

- **You can only hear** an echo if it comes back more than 0.1 sec after the original sound.

- **Sound travels** 111.5ft (34m) in 0.1 sec, so you only hear echoes from surfaces at least 56ft (17m) away.

- **Smooth hard surfaces** give the best echoes because they break up the sound waves the least.

- **Acoustics** is the study of how sounds are created, transmitted, and received.

- **The acoustics** of a space is how sound is heard and how it echoes around that space, whether it is a room or a large concert hall.

- **When concert halls** are designed, the idea is not to eliminate echoes altogether but to use them effectively.

- **A hall with too much echo** sounds harsh and unclear, because echoing sounds interfere with new sounds.

- **A hall without echoes** sounds muffled and lifeless.

- **Even in the best** concert halls, the music can be heard fading after the orchestra stops playing. This delay is called the reverberation time. Concert halls typically have a reverberation time of 2sec. A cathedral may reverberate for up to 8sec, giving a more mellow, but less clear, sound.

Acids and alkalis

◀ Citrus fruits such as oranges, lemons, and limes have a tart taste because they contain a mild acid, called citric acid. It has a pH of 3.

- **Mild acids,** such as acetic acid in vinegar, taste sour .

- **Strong acids,** such as sulphuric acid, are highly corrosive. They dissolve metals.

- **Acids** are solutions that are made when certain substances containing hydrogen dissolve in water.

- **Hydrogen atoms** have a single electron. When acid-making substances dissolve in water, the hydrogen atoms lose their electron and become positively charged

> ★ STAR FACT ★
> Hydrochloric acid in the stomach (with a pH of 1.8) is essential for digestion.

ions. Ions are atoms that have gained or lost electrons.

- **The strength of an acid** depends on how many hydrogen ions form.

- **The opposite of an acid** is a base. Weak bases such as baking powder taste bitter and feel soapy. Strong bases such as caustic soda are corrosive.

- **A base that dissolves** in water is called an alkali. Alkalis contain negatively charged ions—typically ions of hydrogen and oxygen, called hydroxide ions.

- **When you add an acid** to an alkali, the acid is neutralized. The acid and alkali react together forming water and a salt.

- **Chemists** use indicators such as litmus paper to test for acidity. Acids turn litmus paper red. Alkalis turn it blue. The strength of an acid may be measured on the pH scale. The strongest acid (laboratory hydrochloric) has a pH of 1. The strongest alkali has a pH of 14. Pure water has a pH of about 7 and is neutral—neither acid nor alkali.

Solids, liquids, and gases

- **Most substances** can exist in three states: solid, liquid, or gas. These are the states of matter.

- **Substances** change from one state to another at particular temperatures and pressures.

- **As temperature rises,** solids melt to become liquids. As it rises further, liquids evaporate to become gases.

- **The temperature** at which a solid melts is its melting point.

- **The maximum temperature** a liquid can reach before turning to gas is called its boiling point.

- **Every solid has strength** and a definite shape as its molecules are firmly bonded in a rigid structure.

▲ Ice melts to water as heat makes its molecules vibrate faster and faster until the bonds between them eventually break.

- **A liquid has a fixed volume** and takes up the shape of any solid container into which it is poured.

- **A liquid flows** because although bonds hold molecules together, they are loose enough to move over each other, rather like dry sand.

- **A gas** such as air does not have any shape, strength, or fixed volume. This is because its molecules are moving too quickly for any bonds to hold them together.

- **When a gas cools,** its molecules slow down until bonds form between them to create drops of liquid. This process is called condensation.

Nitrogen

- **Nitrogen** is a colorless, tasteless, odorless, inert (unreactive) gas, yet it is vital to life.

- **Nitrogen is** 78.08 percent of the air.

- **Nitrogen** turns liquid at −320.8°F (−196°C) and freezes at 346°F (−210°C).

- **Liquid nitrogen** is so cold that it can freeze organic substances so quickly they suffer little damage.

- **Food such as cheesecakes** and raspberries are preserved by being sprayed with liquid nitrogen.

! NEWS FLASH !
When they die, some people have their bodies frozen with liquid nitrogen in the hope that medical science will one day bring them back to life.

◄ On average 220lb (100kg) of nitrate fertilizer are used on every 2.5 acres of farmland in the world to replace nitrogen taken from the soil by crops.

- **Compounds of nitrogen** and oxygen are called nitrates.

- **Nitrogen and oxygen** compounds are an essential ingredient of the proteins and nucleic acids from which all living cells are made.

- **Lightning makes** 250,000 tons of nitric acid a day. It joins nitrogen and oxygen in the air to make nitrogen oxide.

- **On a long ocean dive,** the extra pressure in a diver's lungs makes extra nitrogen dissolve in the blood. If the diver surfaces too quickly the nitrogen forms bubbles, giving "the bends" which can be painful or even fatal.

Nuclear energy

- **The energy** that binds the nucleus of an atom together is enormous, as Einstein showed.

- **By releasing the energy** from the nuclei of millions of atoms, nuclear power stations and bombs can generate a huge amount of power.

- **Nuclear fusion** is when nuclear energy is released by fusing together small atoms such as deuterium (a kind of hydrogen).

- **Nuclear fusion** is the reaction that keeps stars glowing and gives hydrogen bombs their terrifying power.

- **Nuclear fission** releases energy by splitting the large nuclei of atoms such as uranium and plutonium.

- **To split atomic nuclei** for nuclear fission, neutrons are fired into the nuclear fuel.

- **As neutrons crash** into atoms and split their nuclei, they split off more neutrons. These neutrons bombard other nuclei, splitting off more neutrons that bombard more nuclei. This is called a chain reaction.

- **An atom bomb,** or A-bomb, is one of the two main kinds of nuclear weapon. It works by an explosive, unrestrained fission of uranium-235 or plutonium-239.

- **A hydrogen bomb (H-bomb)** or thermonuclear weapon uses a conventional explosion to fuse the nuclei of deuterium atoms in a gigantic nuclear explosion.

- **The H-bomb** that exploded at Novaya Zemlya in 1961 released 10,000 times more energy than the bombs dropped on Hiroshima, in Japan, in 1945.

► Nuclear fission involves firing a neutron (blue ball) into the nucleus of a uranium or plutonium atom. When the nucleus splits, it fires out more neutrons that split more nuclei, setting off a chain reaction.

Spectrum

▶ When the beam from a flashlight passes through a prism it fans out into a rainbow of colors.

● **A spectrum** is a range of different wavelengths of electromagnetic radiation.

● **The white light of sunlight** can be broken up into its full spectrum of colors with a triangular block of glass called a prism. The prism is set in a dark room and lit only by a shaft of sunlight or similar white light.

● **The prism refracts (bends)** short wavelengths of light more than longer wavelengths, so the light fans out in bands ranging from violet to red.

● **The order of colors** in a spectrum is always: red, orange, yellow, green, blue, indigo, violet.

● **Scientists** remember the order of the colors with the "name"—Roy G. Biv.

● **Infrared** is red light made of waves that are too long for human eyes to see.

● **Ultraviolet** is made of waves that are too short for our eyes to see.

● **Spectroscopy,** or spectral analysis, is the study of the spectrum created when a solid, liquid, or gas glows.

● **Every substance** produces its own unique spectrum, so spectroscopy helps to identify substances.

Energy conversion

● **Energy is measured** in joules (J). One joule is the energy involved in moving a force of 1 newton over 1 meter.

● **A kilojoule (kJ)** is 1,000 joules.

● **A calorie** was the old measure of energy, but is now used only for food: 1 calorie is 4.187J; 1 Cal is 1,000 calories.

● **For scientists,** "work" is the transfer of energy. When you move an object, you do work. The work done is the amount of energy (in joules) gained by the object.

● **For scientists, "power"** is the work rate, or the rate at which energy is changed from one form to another.

● **The power of a machine** is the amount of work it does divided by the length of time it takes to do it.

● **The power of a car's engine** is the force with which the engine turns multiplied by the speed at which it turns.

● **A transducer** is a device for turning an electrical signal into a non-electrical signal (such as sound) or vice versa. A loudspeaker is a transducer.

● **The energy in the Big Bang** was 10^{68} joules. The world's coal reserves are 2×10^{23} joules; a thunderstorm has 10^{14} joules of energy; a large egg has 400,000 joules.

● **When sleeping** you use 60 Cals an hour and 80 Cals when sitting. Running uses 600 Cals. Three hours of reading or watching TV uses 240 Cals. Seven hours' hard work uses about 1,000 Cals—or about 10 eggs' worth.

◀ A hydroelectric power station is a device that converts the energy of moving water into electrical energy.

Calcium

- **Calcium** is a soft, silvery white metal. It does not occur naturally in pure form.

- **Calcium** is the fifth most abundant element on the Earth.

- **Calcium** is one of six alkaline-earth metals.

- **Most calcium compounds** are white solids called limes. They include chalk, porcelain, enamel on teeth, cement, seashells, and the limescale that makes water "hard."

- **The word "lime"** comes from the Latin word for slime.

- **Quicklime** is calcium oxide. It is called "quick" (Old English for "living") because when water drips on it, it twists and swells as if it is alive.

- **Slaked lime** is calcium hydroxide. It may be called "slaked" because it slakes (quenches) a plant's thirst for lime in acid soils.

- **Calcium has** an atomic number of 20. It has a melting point of 1,542°F (839°C) and a boiling point of 2,703°F (1,484°C).

▲ Calcium is one of the basic building materials of living things. It is one of the crucial ingredients in shell and bone, which is why they are typically white.

- **Limelight** was the bright light used by theaters in the days before electricity. It was made by applying a mix of oxygen and hydrogen to pellets of calcium.

- **Calcium adds rigidity** to bones and teeth and helps to control muscles. Your body gets it from milk and cheese.

Oil compounds

▲ In an oil refinery, crude oil is broken down into an enormous range of different hydrocarbons.

- **Hydrocarbons** are compounds made only of carbon and hydrogen atoms. Most oil products are hydrocarbons.

- **The simplest hydrocarbon** is methane, the main gas in natural gas (and flatulence from cows!). Methane molecules are one carbon atom and four hydrogen atoms.

◄ This is a propane molecule. The carbon atoms are purple, the hydrogen atoms are gray.

- **Alkanes or paraffins** are a family of hydrocarbons in which the number of hydrogen atoms is two more than twice the number of carbon atoms.

- **Lighter alkanes** are gases like methane, propane and butane (used in camping stoves). All make good fuels.

- **Candles** contain a mixture of alkanes.

- **Alkenes or olefins** are a family of hydrocarbons in which there are twice as many hydrogen atoms as carbon atoms.

- **The simplest alkene** is ethene, which is used to make polythene and other plastics such as PVC.

- **Green bananas and tomatoes** are often ripened rapidly in ripening rooms filled with ethene.

- **Ethene** is the basis of many paint strippers.

- **Ethene** can be used to make ethanol, the alcohol in alcoholic drinks.

INDEX

Acknowledgments

Artists: Roger Goode (Beehive illustration), Rob Jakeway, Janos Marffy, Martin Sanders,
Mike White (Temple Rogers), John Woodcock

The publishers would like to thank the following sources for the photographs used in this book:

Page 19 (C/R) Science Photo Library; Page 23 (C) Corbis; Page 27 (T/R) The Stock Market; Page 31 (T/L) Science Photo Library;
Page 42 (B/L) The Stock Market; Page 50 (T/R) Science Photo Library.

All other photographs are from MKP Archives